BECOMING A MOTHER

Reflections on Adoptive Parenthood

Mari Gallagher

ORPEN PRESS

Becoming a Mother
by Mari Gallagher

First published in 2018 by
Orpen Press
Top Floor,
Unit K9
Grants Road,
Greenogue Business Park,
Rathcoole,
Dublin,
Ireland.

e-mail: info@orpenpress.com
www.orpenpress.com

ISBN: 978-1-78605-058-8
Epub ISBN: 978-1-78605-059-5

Printed in Dublin, Ireland by SPRINTprint

'It took me a lot longer to become a mother
than it did to adopt a baby.'
Jana Wolff, *Secret Thoughts of an Adoptive Mother*

For Inna and Marina

TABLE OF CONTENTS

A Note from the Author

The adoption referred to in *Becoming a Mother* relates to the adoption of a child from outside of Ireland, known as intercountry adoption. The details and experiences as they relate to intercountry adoption will differ greatly from domestic adoption; that is, a child born in Ireland and adopted by an Irish resident. When adoption is referred to, particularly in the case of search and reunion, it is in relation to intercountry adoption, unless otherwise specified.

Adoption fulfils two individual needs – of those who need parents and those who desire to be parents. Infertility led me to form a family through adoption, and while I acknowledge that many people who have not experienced infertility adopt children, *Becoming a Mother* is written from the viewpoint of adoption after infertility.

I have written with the assumption that all children adopted from abroad know they are adopted and that the adoptive parent will not keep their adoption a secret from them. Whatever about the past, in the case of domestic adoption, a baby can be brought into a family and reared without being told they were adopted. However, when a child joins a family by intercountry adoption, they will usually be older than six months, and the whole process of preparing for their adoption, such as adoption assessment and travelling abroad a number of times pre-adoption, is difficult to conceal. Racial differences, if any, will also mark out a child as not being genetically linked to their adoptive parents. Therefore, when I write about various aspects of adoption, I am writing with the assumption that the child's adoption is not a secret and that openness is embraced by the adoptive parents.

The adopted child and adoptive parent are referred to alternatively as 'he/she' or 'they'. I refer to the birth *mother* rather than the birth *parent*, as in most cases the birth father is either unknown or absent. I do acknowledge this is not always the case and that many birth fathers have been affected by adoption. For ease of reading, I use the acronyms

A Note from the Author

'AP' to denote adoptive parent, 'IA' to denote intercountry adoption and 'ART' to denote assisted reproductive technology. *Becoming a Mother* is my personal experience of adoptive parenthood. Adoption from Russia and Kazakhstan differs in many ways to adoption from other countries, particularly in terms of search and reunion possibilities; it is important to note that I have written *only* from my perspective. While this perspective is my own, and I use a first-person narrative to describe various aspects of my life as an AP, the accurate narrative would be 'we', as without the support and collaboration of my much-loved husband and best friend, Phil, little would have taken place. I take this opportunity to put on the record that Phil's calm and sagacious presence is in everything that happens in this book, as is his tenacity, commitment and all-round brilliance in slogging his way through learning Russian, our children's birth language.

Becoming a Mother has been battering at the edges of my brain for years, demanding to be written. I have been forced to park my demons and remember the words of Dave Eggers: 'Write your goddamned book now. The world awaits.'

FOREWORD

'I speak as a person, from a context of personal experience
and personal learnings.'

Carl Rogers, *On Becoming a Person*

Two decades and more ago, when I was first considering adoption,
I headed straight for the local bookshop. Despite a comprehensive
search in several outlets, there were no adoption books on the shelf.
The parenting section carried a selection of titles to help parents
through the various stages, from babyhood to teens, but the AP was
not catered for as a target market. Nowadays, the click of a mouse will
provide adoption reading-material from a long list of titles. Despite
this, two decades on, and despite almost 50,000 adoptions in Ireland,
there is still a dearth of books for APs in most Irish bookshops. At the
time of my search for adoption reading-material, I would have liked to
have found a book from the perspective of an Irish AP, simply because
in Ireland we have a unique standpoint on adoption, with the record of
illegal adoptions and the links with the infamous Magdalene Laundries
creating an overhang. Secrecy and silence still pervades adoption and
consequently, many of the nuances surrounding adoption are misunderstood and misinterpreted. *Becoming a Mother* is written, then, for the
purpose of answering the questions that filled my head when I first set
out on the road to adoption, the main question being: 'What does it
mean to be an adoptive parent in Ireland?'

I strive to answer this question by examining the complexity of
adoptive parenting, with a focus on intercountry adoptive parenting,
as well as looking at adoption from three perspectives: the adopted
person, the birth parent and the adoptive parent; this is also known as
the 'adoption triad'. Extensive reading of adoption literature (bought
online!) and attendance over the years at numerous adoptive parenting

workshops have taught me about adoption and helped me to deal with the challenges of adoptive parenting. Reading has really helped me to unravel adoption's mysteries and intricacies. Thanks to the courage of adopted people, birth mothers and adoptive mothers who have generously shared their stories, those of us in the midst of child-rearing have been able to gain precious insights. It's hard to argue with what comes from the horse's mouth; the adopted person is the one who bought the T-shirt and wore it. The adopted person's experience is the incontrovertible proof of what adoption really involves.

I Never Thought it Would Be Like This

When the momentous decision was made to apply to the Health Board (now the HSE) to be assessed for adoption, I assumed that if a child was adopted as an infant, it would be almost the same as if the child was born to me. After all, what would they know or realise about what happened to them if they were a mere baby when relinquishment happened? I have no memory of my time as a baby, so how could they remember anything? I was quite sure that a child adopted as a baby would not carry any 'baggage' and would not suffer as much as an older child who witnessed and was party to their relinquishment. However, the impact of adoption on the adopted person was something that came as a shock to me. The impact of my children's relinquishment has infiltrated all aspects of my life as an AP and has driven me to learn as much as possible about the complexities of adoption. Also, it is important to say that this book deals with the adoption of a child as an infant, as this was my experience of adoption. Much of what I have written about attachment and other aspects of adoption will vary in the case of the adoption of an older child.

More is required of me than simply unconditional love of my children. I have had to prise adoption apart in order to learn everything about the most important people in my life. Becoming a mother by adoption is different to giving birth. While this seems like stating the obvious, the differences between parenting by biology (linked by blood) and adoption (linked by love and law) are what make adoptive parenting in equal parts fascinating and painful. I write about the differences – the starkest being the balancing of the pain felt by your children through their loss of blood ties, and the pain felt by you through your loss of blood ties. In the midst of all those opposing feelings is the child's birth history and the void created by relinquishment, the filling of which is the AP's greatest challenge.

Like fate, destiny and all else uncontrollable in life, our children through adoption will have been born in all manner of circumstances. Embracing their birth history, digesting it and dissembling it has been for me one of the most difficult and rewarding aspects of being an AP. Adoption starts by a birth mother making a life-changing decision about the future of her child. Another mother's decision was the basis for my motherhood. An indelible, significant part of my child's life was lived before they came to me. These are the incontrovertible facts of adoption. It is entirely natural that my child will want to find out about the missing piece of their life. One of the most common themes from my reading of adopted people's writing is the hurt of not being linked with their birth history. 'My history was stolen from me' is a frequent statement in the blogs, books and articles published by adopted people throughout the world. This is an invaluable message for APs and one that is explored in detail in Chapter Seven: Search and Reunion – A Blood Trail.

Becoming a Mother was also inspired by a question posed a few years ago by my daughter: 'How come nobody understands adoption?' Tatiana had shared her feelings about her adoption with a few of her (non-adopted) friends and was struggling with what she interpreted as a lack of understanding. This book is an attempt to explore the many complexities of adoption in the hope that more people will 'get' what's going on when an adopted person shares their feelings.

Adoption Is an Intensely Private Matter

Writing a book on the personal experience of adoption automatically contradicts the statement that adoption is an intensely private matter. Therefore, for obvious reasons, personal anecdotes relating to my children will be recounted in a general, non-specific way. This book is a point-in-time account of lives in progress like any other, and adoption is only one part of what we are. Every morning I wake and give endless thanks for the incomparable, immeasurable joy for the miracle of the children in my life.

INTRODUCTION

Most people have an opinion on the subject of adoption, depending on what their own personal experience has been. We might know someone who has struggled to become pregnant and who – together with their partner – have embarked on the long and demanding route to adoption. Some of us know a birth mother who has faced the unimaginable sadness of parting with her baby in order for it to be raised by someone else. We may be familiar with the challenges of adopted children and adults in developing an understanding of who they are and coming to terms with the loss of their birth family and birth country. It is really only those who have lived these experiences who are the real experts on adoption.

Since 1991, over 5,000 children have been adopted to Ireland from forty-one different countries around the world – countries as diverse as Uzbekistan, Thailand, Ethiopia and China. These children join more than 44,000 children and adults who were born and adopted here in Ireland. All of these children, their birth families and their adoptive families have their own fascinating stories to tell.

However, not many of these stories have been written, and that is why Mari Gallagher's is so welcome. Mari's story tells of the pain of longing for motherhood through to the meeting with her beautiful son and daughter in Russia and Kazakhstan respectively. She describes the challenges and joys of meeting the particular needs of adopted children, from practical attachment parenting to helping them find out important birth information.

Barnardos provides post adoption support to adoptive parents and their children, as well as to Irish birth mothers and adopted adults. We are most grateful to Mari for the support she is providing to Barnardos through the proceeds of her book.

Christine Hennessey, 4 April 2018
Project Leader of Barnardos Post Adoption Service

Chapter One

An Overview of Adoption

'Adoption is not an exact science.'
Evelyn Burns Robinson, *Adoption and Loss: The Hidden Grief*

Adoption encompasses many primal and contrasting aspects of the human psyche: the profound importance of identity; the impact of nature versus nurture; the overwhelming power of love, attachment and how it affects personality; the need to know birth history; the politics of family dynamics; the reality of not being able to continue the birth line; the danger of keeping secrets; and on and on.

Little wonder people have long been obsessed with adoption and the many complex streams that flow through it. Stories proliferate with adoption as the central theme or as an important subplot. Classic novels such as *Jane Eyre*, *Oliver Twist*, *Matilda* and *The Jungle Book* feature adoption as a central topic. In recent times, more movies and television series have begun to include subplots involving adoption: *This is Us*, *Mad Men*, *In Treatment*, *The Legacy*, *Juno*, *The Blind Side* and *Despicable Me*, to name but a few. Indeed, after watching many movies and TV dramas that weaved adoption into the plot, it seemed as if a story was not complete without adoption featuring somewhere.

At the core of adoption is the search for identity. You could say the search for identity is at the core of being human. Which of us, despite being surrounded by a biological family, has not spent some time searching for who we are? The question of 'who am I?' has been posed time and time again. Adoption is then a metaphor for everyone. If searching for oneself is an integral part of humanity, and searching for oneself is an integral part of being adopted, then it follows that the experience of adoption represents humanity at its most raw and authentic.

An Overview of Adoption

Adoption is defined (as per the Adoption Authority of Ireland [the AAI]) as: 'The permanent transfer of parental rights and duties from the birth parents to the adoptive parents. An adopted child is considered to be the child of the adopters as if born to them in wedlock.' Almost 50,000 members of the Irish population are adopted, either Irish-born or born outside of the country (Adoption Authority of Ireland, Annual Report 2016), although anecdotal evidence suggests the figure is nearer to 90,000 (Lawless, 2016). When all those 'touched by adoption' are included in that grouping (APs, birth parents, adoptive grandparents, aunts, uncles, siblings, etc.), the figure is closer to half a million, or an estimated 10 percent of Irish residents; a sizeable chunk of the Irish population is linked in some way to adoption.

In *Love's Promises*, Martha M. Ertman estimates there are between 120,000 and 150,000 adoptions a year in the US. 'The numbers get really big when you realize that for every adoption, adoptive and birth families also are deeply affected. According to one estimate, fully 60 percent of Americans have been personally touched by adoption' (2015, p. 78).

Adoption Terminology

Adoption Triad or Adoption Triangle

The adoption triad (or triangle) describes the main parties of adoption, namely: birth parent, adopted person (adoptee) and adoptive parent (AP).

Touched by Adoption

Touched by adoption describes those impacted by adoption. The expression has been used in adoption writing to denote immediate parties in the adoption triad: the birth mother, the adopted person and the AP as well as those linked to the adopted person: parents of adoptive and birth parents, non-adopted siblings of adoptees, uncles and aunts of adopted people, birth siblings of adoptees and the children of adoptees. Few family members are left untouched by adoption. As the adoptee grows up and has children, those children may ask questions about their parent's birth history. The spread of adoption's tentacles around the family unit must be acknowledged as it encompasses a wide hinterland.

Closed Adoption

Also known as secret or confidential adoption, closed adoption is a process whereby the record of the birth parents' details is kept sealed. Often the birth father's details are not recorded, even on the birth certificate. A closed adoption means there is no contact between the birth parents and the adoptive family after the adoption takes place until such time as both parties agree to such contact.

Open Adoption

This refers to contact and/or the sharing of information between the birth mother and APs before and/or after placement of the child and continuing for the life of the child.

Paradoxes and Dichotomy

Adoption is a fundamental life-altering event. Loss and heartache is experienced by all parties involved in the adoption triangle. Unfortunately, society generally encourages birth parents, adoptees and adoptive parents to ignore their losses. Adoptive parents are expected to be happy to have a child, adoptees perhaps experience that they ought to be grateful that they were adopted as opposed to have grown up in state care or an orphanage in a different country, a 'a third-world country'. Birth parents also are urged to forget their loss or made to feel that they do not deserve to feel their loss (Silverstein and Kaplan, 1982).

Adoption represents loss from three different viewpoints: the birth mother who relinquishes her child, the adopted child who is separated from their birth mother and the AP who has been unable to give birth. Silverstein and Kaplan accurately describe this loss:

Without loss there is no adoption. Birth parents lose the child to whom they are genetically connected (possibly forever), adoptees experience their first loss when separated from their birth mother/birth family and with that they lose a significant part of their personal history which is crucial for a grounded identity. Adoptive parents lose the child that would have been born to them, through infertility, failed pregnancy, stillbirth, or the death of a child and therefore have suffered great loss prior to adoption (1982).

The adopted people who have told their stories project adoption from the point of view of the person left behind, severed from their birth right. APs view adoption as proof of their desire to parent and the substantiation of an intense, innate primal need. Birth parents (mostly birth mothers) view the loss of their child as a lifelong, unending heartbreak and their efforts to resume contact as laden with obstacles. APs and birth parents stand on either side of adoption – one party gains from the other's loss.

Barbara Katz Rothman details the dichotomy: 'As a public policy, adoption cannot be the long-range solution for infertility, even though it obviously works for many individuals. It does not work as a social policy because it makes us dependent on the grief of one group of people to solve the problems of another group of people' (1989, p. 86).

Books, newspaper articles and blogs written by members of the adoption triad illustrate the opposing sides of the adoption spectrum and the dichotomy at its heart. This dichotomy is further accentuated by the ongoing campaign of prospective adopters to change laws that, from their perspective, thwart international adoption (IA).

Prospective adopters protest in articles and social groups about the pain and injustice of political and administrative restrictions as they attempt to adopt children from institutional care into a loving home. On the other hand, birth-mother groups write blogs and books about the pain and injustice of being forced by societal mores to relinquish their child, whom they have never stopped mourning. Campaigning birth mothers insist that adoption is not in the best interests of the child and should be abolished, with every possible effort made to keep birth mother and child together. Adopted adults write autobiographies and form online groups railing at the pain and injustice inflicted on them by the adoption process as they search for their birth history.

These contradictory goals within the adoption triangle illustrate the complexity of adoption. Uttering the words 'I was adopted' or 'they were adopted' generates a bittersweet mix of emotions. The image of the intense desire of the APs to give nurturing love coalesced with the tragedy of a woman walking away from her baby is paradoxical. This image is another illustration of the complexity of adoption. That the word 'adoption' itself can evoke such emotive and opposing images is testament to its complexity. Even after twenty years of adoptive parenthood, when the word is said, I find myself wincing, my ears pricking up, my senses on high alert, waiting to hear what is to be said and hyper aware of my own sensitivity to the topic.

An Array of Images and Viewpoints

Depending on how you are touched by adoption or in what era you were born, the word can evoke a pastiche of images and scenarios: Magdalene Laundries, stolen babies, fallen women, grasping adopters, baby trade, loss of heritage and blood links, birth family search, relinquished babies, campaigning prospective adopters, unwanted pregnancies, devastating infertility, grieving birth mothers, grieving infertile women, neglectful birth mothers, angry adoptees and overwhelmed APs. A diverse pastiche indeed! Every image and scenario are actual and authentic. Every image and scenario are equally characterised by grief and loss for the parties concerned. The image evoked by the word 'adoption' depends where in the triad you stand; that is, whether you are an adopted person, birth mother or AP, or someone who is connected to a member of the triad.

To make adoption happen, a woman had to give away her child. The child was severed from their genetic family. Historically, the connotations around relinquishment are many. The single mother, pregnant outside of wedlock, forced by societal mores to relinquish her child as she could not consider raising them alone, is an emblem of pre-modern Ireland. The addressing of the perceived 'plight' of the single mother is the driver for the existence of institutions in Ireland such as the Magdalene Laundries and the deluge of suffering experienced by women whose babies were illegally removed and sent abroad for adoption. More recently, in Great Britain for instance, children have been removed from parents who have been found to be neglecting or abusing those children and subsequently adopted without birth parental consent. The children are still afforded monitored contact with their birth parents (Oakwater, 2012).

Societal Progress – The Hague Convention and Intercountry Adoption (IA)

Societal progress has thankfully led to changed attitudes toward birth outside of marriage and, consequently, fewer children are being placed for adoption. Domestic adoption in recent decades has been a rare occurrence in Ireland, and the enactment of the Adoption Act 1991 gave IA a statutory base. Since 1991, over 5,000 children born outside of Ireland were placed for adoption in Ireland (Adoption Authority of Ireland, Annual Report 2016). Since 2010 (the year of ratification of The Hague Convention), the number of children adopted in Ireland through IA has plummeted. The Hague Convention of 29 May 1993 on the Protection of Children and Co-operation in Respect of Intercountry Adoption was ratified by Ireland in 2010. The convention was established to ensure the highest standards in IA. It contains stipulations such as the rigorous assessment of prospective adopters, recommendations of counselling for relinquishing parents and accreditation requirements for adoption intermediaries to protect against child trafficking. The convention has a number of principal features, one of which is called the 'Subsidiarity Principle'. This refers to the aspiration that a child should be 'raised by his or her birth family or extended family whenever possible […] as a general rule, institutional care should be considered as a last resort for children (www.hcch.net).

Emily Logan, former (Ireland) Ombudsman for Children, in a radio interview in 2012 where she was discussing the appeal by prospective Irish APs to lobby for bi-lateral agreements to facilitate IA, described IA as a 'last resort for children'. Ms Logan's description of IA as a last resort rather than institutional care (as outlined in The Hague Convention) exemplified the general negativity towards IA.

The negative press coverage of IA mainly centres on the perceived wrongness of the taking of a child out of their country of origin, even if that child is being reared in an institution in their native country. APs are perceived as willing to separate a child from their heritage and culture in order to fulfil a primal desire to become a parent. Many have accused APs of fuelling international 'baby trade' by adopting children from institutions around the world. Why not, asks the accusers, use the expenses paid to the adoption agency to instead support the birth mother and thus allow her to keep her child? If the welfare of the child is the priority, then why not prioritise the keeping of a child with their mother? Why not use the superior spending power of APs to help a woman in dire need instead of severing the child from its mother for the AP's benefit?

Some of the most vocal opposers of IA are adult intercountry adoptees who state that IA is skewed in favour of the adopters: a child sacrifices their heritage and chance of reunion with blood relatives so that the adult can be 'cured' of infertility. Adult intercountry adoptees describe childhoods where they were deprived of information about or consideration of their racial identities by adoptive parents who were dismissive of the child's birth history.

Georgiana A. Macavei, a Romanian-born adoptee raised in America, writes: 'I was expected to be just like my adoptive "family", but I looked and acted nothing like them. I had my own history that was never to be discussed… It has been difficult to be a foreigner here. Adoption is no guarantee of a "better" life. The search for myself seems never-ending' (2014, p. 27).

Peter F. Dodds, born in Germany and raised in America, in an article published in an independent online journal, *Sociology Between the Gaps: Forgotten and Neglected Topics*, draws parallels between IA and slavery. The parallels being that both slavery and adoption are responses to needs – the need for labour by rich people and the need to form a family by (rich) infertile couples; both slave and foreign adoptee are perceived as better off than those left behind and both slavery and adoption are classified as a 'common Christian calling' (2015).

Daniel Ibn Zayd, born in Lebanon and raised in America, writes in 2012 that: 'Adoption is, in and of itself, a violence based in inequality. It is candy-coated, marketed, and packaged to seemingly concerned families and children, but it is an economically and politically incentivized crime' (p. 217).

Illegal adoptions involving the exchange of money in return for children has further tainted IA. In the majority of international adoptions, the birth parents of the children are still alive, albeit unable to care for their children. The term 'orphan' and 'orphanage' is used but is not accurate in relation to the majority of children adopted from abroad. Most of the children adopted are not orphans but children of living birth parents who saw no other option but to place their child in institutional care due to their extreme economic deprivation or political upheaval.

In *Beyond Good Intentions: A Mother Reflects on Raising Internationally Adopted Children*, Cheri Register, AP to two Korean-born daughters, suggests that an assumption of superiority underpins the act of IA: the child is better off out of their birth country and better off in their adoptive country because their birth country is a 'hellhole'. Register writes that 'Reminders of my child's good fortune never cease. These reminders (by friends and family) arise out of a self-assured nationalism that without question ranks your country as better than her birthplace' (2005, p.126). Register then ponders what would have happened had her daughter been able to make a choice: 'What if it had been up to her? Would she have chosen this country or some other, and how would it feel not to be uprooted at all, but to be a citizen of Korea?' (p. 130).

Intercountry Adoption – The Right Thing for the Child?

Despite the benefits bestowed to the child of being lifted out of institutional care and the subsequent joy of becoming a mother to two beautiful children, I have harboured reservations about whether taking children out of their native countries and giving them homes thousands of miles away from their heritage is inherently the *right thing*.

These arguments have rattled my brain for long periods of time, generating guilt and defensiveness in equal measure, as well as a few questions of my own. If donations were made to families, instead of the payment of fees to adoption agencies, could I be sure that the families would receive the money? If the respective governments of Russia and Kazakhstan, the countries in which my children were born, were not able or willing to set up a social welfare system that supported families in need, and if placing children in institutional care was the only option, how then could I be sure that money sent by me to these countries would even be directed toward the birth family in need? While the suggestion that APs should donate to the countries concerned rather than pay agencies to link them with children who need to be adopted is well-intentioned, there is no guarantee that donations would be directed toward needy birth mothers and allow them to keep their children.

The reality is that, despite what the opposers say, children will continue to be abandoned by parents who, for a variety of reasons, are unable to look after them. The International Adoption Association stated in 2014 that there are roughly 17,900,000 orphans worldwide who are living in orphanages or on the streets, although it is impossible to accurately gauge numbers.

A 2012 article in the *Moscow Times* entitled 'How Many Kids in Institutions? No Way to Know' by Howard Amos and Jennifer Rankin outlined the lack of official data in relation to the numbers of children in institutional care in Russia. According to UNICEF, countries of the former Soviet Union and the Warsaw Pact (Albania, Bulgaria, Czechoslovakia, Hungary, Poland, Romania and West Germany; the pact dissolved in 1991) continue to have the highest rates of institutionalization in the world. In 2010, while Russia was still eligible to allow children to be adopted by people from outside the country, the numbers in institutions were estimated at 260,000. By any reasonable estimate, this number will now have increased, given that adoption is no longer an option. At the time of writing (February 2017), 1,607 children in Ireland have been adopted from Russia (AAI Annual Report, 2016).

The authorities in countries such as Russia who have not signed up to The Hague Convention see it as preferable to neglect children by leaving them in institutional care rather than to step out of denial and allow these children the chance of being reared in a loving home, even if it is thousands of miles away. More enlightened attitudes and efficient methods of communication have rendered the world a smaller place. Search and reunion in IA is not the impossible improbability it once was.

No matter how much adoption is attacked, parents, tragically, will continue to be unable to rear their children, and those children will continue to be placed into institutional care and languish there if adoption is not possible.

A childhood in institutional care followed by a release onto the streets at age sixteen without the guidance of an adult mentor is the fate in store for institutionalised children who are not adopted. The downsides of being reared in institutional care have been well documented, and flourishing conditions of attachment and sensory processing disorders due to the absence of individual love and attention often manifest. It is hard to see how opposers to IA would see being reared in an institution preferable to being adopted into a loving home, even if that home is thousands of miles away.

Despite the negativity imbuing adoption and my own reservations about the *rightness* of IA, the overarching image of adoption for me, an AP, is joy and fulfilment for a previously childless couple – a devoted mother and father bringing up a child whom they strive to provide with roots and wings.

Chapter Two

A Primal Desire

'The motives for giving birth are probably not much
different from the motives for adopting.'
Cheri Register, *Are Those Kids Yours?*

What Came Before

The primal desire to parent is an integral part of adoptive parenthood.
In order to explore adoptive parenthood, an understanding is necessary of what went on in the AP's life *before* the adoption of the child
and in particular, the impact of not being able to bear a child. Involuntary childlessness induces shame, particularly in a society obsessed
with family and child-rearing. E. Wayne Carp writes of the emotional
quagmire that is involuntary childlessness:

> The baby boom, beginning in the mid 1940s and reaching its
> peak in the late 1950s, with its dramatic rise in marriages and
> births, exacerbated the increased demand for adults to adopt
> and resulted in adoption agencies being inundated with requests
> for children. Parenthood during the Cold War became a patri-
> otic necessity. Many childless couples sought adoption in record
> numbers as one solution to their shame of infertility. Obsession
> with parenthood led to the marginalization of the childless in
> unprecedented ways (1998, p. 29).

Carp also writes about the anger of prospective APs as they struggled
to adopt:

Frustrated couples blamed adoption agencies, not the scarce supply of infants, for their inability to find a child. Their hostility toward adoption agencies was fed in part by popular magazines. Articles reported that one million children languished in institutions while social workers dithered. Prospective adoptive couples, turned down by adoption agencies, lashed out at the apparent injustice. One young woman succinctly captured childless couples' resentment of and antagonism toward adoption agencies: 'These agency people are all trying to play God – and beat him at his own game' (1998, p. 29).

Shame induced by childlessness combined with a primal desire to parent is an explosive load to bear. The journey to adoptive parenthood is filled with anxiety and uncertainty. This is my story of what came before.

You Have No Conception

Not all parenthood starts with the desire to parent. Adoptive parenthood definitely does. Longing for parenthood didn't hit me until my early thirties when I had already become, in stark medical terminology, an elderly primigravida, the unforgiving term for those who delayed getting pregnant until they were 35 years old. Until I reached my early thirties, my maternal urge was non-existent: there were too many other things to do, too strong a need to become secure and confident in my job, too many parts of the world to visit and too many parts of myself that I needed to straighten out.

I had observed enough of parenthood to decide that it equalled stress and extra responsibility: my mother, declaring with her trademark honesty, that rearing children was 'hard work'; other people's children who whined constantly and demanded attention; work colleagues who arrived in bleary-eyed and pale from lack of sleep; and friends whose lives had shrunk as soon as they became parents. Mostly though, without having met *the one*, parenthood was not going to be for me. It does take two after all, and I never saw myself in the single-mother role. Some women from an early age long for motherhood. For me, the yearning did not start until I was 34, married for two years, and it hit, all at once, like a super-fast freight train. The discovery of my infertility, albeit unexplained, was the ultimate confidence trick. I had carefully protected myself against pregnancy because I wasn't ready. Now, the time was right, and I was ready; my body, as it drifted toward the dreaded 35, had other ideas.

Trying to conceive was a type of madness, a 'mad cow' disease during which years of my dwindling fertility spun frantically past, months in which my life, measured in terms of fecundity and ever-arriving monthly periods, disappeared faster than ever before. I was being denied an absolute, natural right. Not getting pregnant was the great leveller: there was no discrimination against class, social behaviour, status or general ability. It didn't matter how much you had achieved in your life, whether you were solvent, well educated, physically healthy, mentally stable, a pillar of the community, a potentially loving parent or any of the opposites of the aforementioned. Anyone, anywhere, at any time, could be the one who ended up infertile. Getting pregnant consumed me. I was stuck, unable to plan or move forward. My entire being screamed the frustration of unutilised maternal love. Gloria Frym's words capture my screams: 'I want to bear! To bear! But the birds of loss have made a nest here' (1989, p. 145). During the years I spent trying to conceive, getting pregnant became the height of my ambitions. Because I couldn't achieve it, despite my best efforts, it turned into the ultimate elusive goal.

Anger

Angry, resentful questions took over me. Where did all this stuff about getting pregnant after intercourse come from? How can it be that you have sex *every* day of the week for umpteen months in succession and *not* become pregnant? How can that be possible? Around me, in my obsessed-with-getting-pregnant frame of mind, it seemed that women careless with their health or unconcerned about whether or not they could actually rear a child were easily reproducing. Infertility did not discriminate. Equally, women careful with their health, fit and highly educated were easily reproducing. A diagnosis of my 'unexplained' infertility, meaning there was nothing wrong that could be pin-pointed, was made. Clearly there *was* something wrong or I would be pregnant.

Infertility dominated all my thoughts. A sizeable chunk of my desperation was driven by the realisation that I had functioned all my life under the assumption that fertility was a given. The very thought of getting pregnant outside of marriage had petrified me during my teens and twenties. What was all that about I now asked myself? I reflected on how I had 'minded myself', a 'good Catholic' girl avoiding the horrific 'shame trap' of single motherhood, chastely batting off sexual advances even when they were coming from desirable men.

'I could get pregnant, what would you do then?' was my profound question to knocked-back Lotharios, dowsing cold water on their ardour. My abstemious prudence seemed presumptuous and pointless in the wisdom of hindsight. Now I was longing for the very result I had so stolidly steered away from for all those years – proof of sexual activity in pregnancy – and it resolutely eluded me.

The spectre of childlessness hung over me, breeding a gamut of emotions: disappointment, isolation, anger, jealousy, frustration and depression. It didn't take much to trigger a spiral into blackness. I spent my time tip-toeing around my own emotions. When a new work colleague or customer politely enquired if I had 'family', as they often would, the impact of having to respond by shaking my head and avoiding their eyes would dull my voice and slow my work pace for the rest of the day. Enunciating my 'failed sexuality' was like a stab to the heart. An acquaintance announced their good news and I struggled to congratulate them, glumness paralysing me.

The greatest thing was the shock. I had always believed that to really try at something was to guarantee success. 'I will give this everything,' I told myself. 'It will come good, I *will* get pregnant.' Acceptance of my infertility and my lack of control over it was the most difficult thing. I had to climb down from my high horse of self-belief into the realisation that not everything I strove for was achievable.

The World of ART (Assisted Reproductive Technology)

'The clock is ticking.' These were the first words from my gynaecologist. Afterwards, I forged a great working relationship with him, but at that moment, his opening gambit far from impressed me.

'The clock is ticking,' he repeated, referring to my recent 35th birthday.

I wanted to swing for him. What a horrible expression! As if I could do anything to stop the march of time. My visit to him was the preamble for my journey into the world of Assisted Reproductive Technology (ART). Along the way I developed a new language – the language of ART – *hysterosalpingogram, intrauterine insemination, clomifene, human chorionic gonadotropin, in vitro fertilisation and gamete intra-fallopian transfer.

If anything had the whiff of a confidence trick off it, then ART was it – apart, of course, from the myth that having lots of sex would get me pregnant. All this voodoo palaver, just to do what men and women have been doing behind sheds, under bushes, in the reclining seats of cars, in seedy motels, and of course bedrooms, since the beginning of time.

ART epitomised all that was woeful about attempting to 'cure' infertility. You feel like you have to give it a try or you'll never forgive yourself in years to come. Yet, I knew, deep down in my soul, that something so brutal, painful and invasive could not, would not, get me pregnant. I had a strong suspicion from the outset that conception requiring the bloodthirsty activities of ART – progesterone injections, mucous and hormone-level checks, blood-giving, lap and dye, laparoscopy, ovulation induction, ultrasound scans, egg collection, embryo transfer – substituted for the sweet, loving intimacy of sex, could NOT get me pregnant. It was all too physically abusive.

Yet I did it, despite the miserable 25 percent success rate. I endured the constant, relentless blood testing, the endless visits to the hospital, the work pressures from taking time off, the perpetual invasion of my intimate body parts – all of which was accompanied by searing stomach pain, bloating, constipation and headaches. I kept my chin up, worked hard on my positive attitude and told myself I was certain to be one of the successful people in the 25 percent bracket.

Broken-Hearted by ART

With the first treatment of IVF under my belt, the culmination of weeks of drug-taking, injections, blood testing, scans, producing eggs (I had eight!) followed by the placing of mixed sperm and eggs (embryo) inside me was finished, and I was back in the world, out and about. Waiting.

Indications that it hadn't worked could hit anywhere, anytime: during a game of tennis (should I even have been playing post-IVF?), in the cinema, in a hardware store as I browsed the shelves. The gremlins would commence in my lower abdomen, pinpricks of pain against my insides. I prayed it was the embryo affixing itself to me, starting to grow, blending obdurately with my body. In the aforementioned hardware store, I dropped my basket of items beside the check out and dashed home. The sight of my period was enough to push me into the depths of darkness.

'How much more of this can I take?' was the question forming in my head.

The prospect of never becoming a mother loomed large. I sought out the biographies of childless women I admired. The wonderful actress Helen Mirren, star of the compelling series, *Prime Suspect*, was one such woman. My childhood heroine, Charlotte Brontë, creator of my life-long favourite character, Jane Eyre, was another. Both women lived in different centuries and managed to live (and Helen Mirren still lives) interesting and productive lives, *sans* children. I tried to convince myself that childfree was a type of lifestyle, not a handicap. I read a book called *Sweet Grapes* by Jean and Michael Carter, which made the case for the positives of a childfree life. The Carters wrote about finding 'a door to the path that can lead the infertile couple to stop being infertile and start living again' (1989, p. 9). The starting to live again involved fewer financial burdens due to not having the expense of rearing a child, leading directly to more freedom with career choices as well as being able to contribute more to the community and the creative arts. The Carters also questioned the existence of maternal instinct, ideas of innate desire and the need to reproduce. While I agreed with the wisdom of their arguments, I wasn't ready to make the move to acceptance of a life without children. The turmoil in my head could only be described as unfulfilled maternal instinct, no matter what the psychologists said. I parked the tenets of the Carters' writing in the 'pending' section of my mind. 'I'll read the book again if the worst happens,' I told myself as I shoved the paperback to the back of the bookcase.

Getting pregnant lodged itself as a firm goal which hijacked my brain and kept me in a perpetual haze of brooding questioning – the most profound question being whether my ovaries were trying to tell me something. I began to wonder if it wasn't meant to be, if I unconsciously was not cut out for motherhood, if my gynaecological make-up was sending me a message – *you do not have what it takes to nurture a child*. I started to ponder about whether something deep in my psyche didn't want to produce a child, some reluctance reaching across and squeezing my ovaries so tight they were unable to perform their function. Maybe I had left it too late – I was in my late twenties before I met the man of my dreams, so technically it wasn't anything I had actually *done*, apart from being unfortunate enough to be a late starter.

The word 'barren' was like a punch to the stomach, so incisively did it describe how I saw my reproductive system – a dry, sandy, empty desert stretching for miles.

The Pain of Injustice

While in the throes of ART, sharp reminders of the injustice of it all littered my day. Fertility-boosting injections done before work, plaster furtively whipped off my arm before getting to my desk in the bank, my first client was a 22-year-old girl who was applying for a small personal loan. I was helping her complete the questionnaire and came to the question: 'How many dependants?' For me, in my craving, childless state, any mention of 'dependants' was like a kick to a sore spot. I asked the question and tears suddenly oozed from my client like a sprinkler. Could her tearful response to the 'how many dependants?' question possibly mean she was going through infertility agony as well? She was more than ten years younger than me, so logistically, it was unlikely.

'I'm pregnant,' she sobbed, her face crumpling.

I wrestled with a box of tissues behind the desk, placing them in front of her. She pulled out a bunch.

'What wonderful news,' I said.

What else would a conception-consumed, baby-longing manikin say? In my world, all pregnant women had to be imbued with endless ecstasy. They had achieved what years of sex, and now medication, hadn't for me. Alarmingly, my words induced heavier torrents and what sounded like a mumbled 'It's not.'

She wiped her eyes before squeezing them shut, shook her head, stared at the desk and went silent in a clear indication that all further discussion on the matter was at an end. The space between us swayed in an existential cloud of yin and yang. Two opposites facing each other over a desk of red tape; the battling, yearning-filled barrenness versus the brimming but unwillingly fecund.

I quickly completed the form and apart from asking her to sign, I spoke little for the rest of the interview. When I shook her warm little hand, her fingers curled away from me, her eyes avoiding mine as she walked away. For ages afterwards, I couldn't stop thinking about her. Our meeting was a symbol of the contra-synchronicity of life, of the goddamn unfairness of it all. A 36-year-old, happily married, financially secure, fairly sane (I hoped) individual with unrequited maternal longing oozing from her pores, who has spent years doing without result what comes naturally to most women.

And here was this young girl, for whom turning pregnant, in her mind, anyway, was a cause for sorrow. I didn't meet her again after that and I don't know how she dealt with her situation. My interaction with her reminded me that life operates in an endless circle of opposing ends of joy and sorrow. Truly one man's (or woman's) paradise is another's hell.

To further reinforce my perception of the injustice of it all, apathetic parenting was everywhere – or so it seemed to my high-alert, unfulfilled, nurturing antennae. Parents who appeared to take for granted their ability to have children were a source of deep irritation. I was throwing my heart and soul into becoming a parent and was coming away empty-handed. As far as I could see, many parents acted as if parenthood was some kind of torture. The reality of the grind of parenting was something I, as an obsessed wannabe, did not yet understand.

My desire to get there coupled with the dread of imminent failure overshadowed any possible downsides. While in the throes of longing to nurture, all actuality went out the window. Becoming a parent was the nirvana and everywhere I went I saw living examples of what I viewed as ingratitude. Parents with glum faces, hunched disconsolately over pushers, shouting 'hurry up' with barely concealed contempt at toddlers and older kids. Once, while walking through a shopping centre car park at lunchtime, I saw a young woman sitting on a bench, flanked by three small children. Two little girls cavorted and chased each other around the bench, every now and then bending down to scoop jelly babies from a spilt packet on the muddy, litter-strewn ground. The smallest, a boy, emitted a nasal, gurgling whinge and attempted to climb up on his mother. He clasped the lapels of his mother's jacket, his arms straining towards her neck. She wound her cigarette-holding arm in the air and yelled 'get off me', jerking him to one side. A loud wail erupted. I scuttled past, unable to witness any more, too suffused with the pain of injustice.

Another day in the supermarket aisle, a family passed me in the frozen food section, the father carrying a toddler, the mother pushing a trolley with a little boy clinging to the handle. The little boy's voice was a monotone whine, his feet intermittently dragging and stomping. The father's unshaven face was creased with exhaustion, his mouth drooping. The mother's hair was tousled and greasy, her expression gloomy, her anorak swinging open to reveal creased leggings and a baggy, stained jumper. Without even looking in the whimpering boy's direction, the father snapped 'Shut up, Gavin.' Why were they not over the moon with joy? I wondered. They have two beautiful children, why are they not smiling from ear to ear?

In the cocoon of my disappointment, I could not countenance parenthood being anything but the harbinger of unfettered joy. Nothing would convince me that perennial sunny-side-up thankfulness was not the default status of being fertile. How could anyone not be dancing jigs of appreciation for being lucky enough to be able to give birth? Yet, parents with miserable faces were everywhere.

To compound my sense of being the victim of gross injustice, physical punishment was often witnessed by me during this time. How could anyone slap children, I pondered. In my perennially long-ing-for-maternity condition, it was bad enough that bearing a child was eluding me, but people I deemed successful due to having attained something that eluded me were further rubbing my nose in it by being physically violent to their offspring. The grind of parenthood and the stress that the demands of childrearing can induce had not entered into my frame of reference.

An incident while on holidays in Greece with my other half at the height of fertility investigations has stayed with me. We were in a restaurant and seated at a table adjacent to a large family group. In their midst, a foursome of young boys, all aged seven or eight, were horsing around with each other. The father sharply admonished the boys a few times for being noisy, but the horseplay continued. The father then stretched his muscular arm and with full strength, whacked one of the small boys squarely across the back of the head. A stunned silence ensued as the child's head bounced forward toward his plate. Within a minute or two, the laughter and chatting at the table re-commenced. The children, however, including the slapped boy, remained silent, clearly cowed by the grim message sent out by the very public punishment. Amidst the conviviality of the restaurant, the banshee-like whimpers of the slapped boy persisted, his little head hanging over his uneaten food for the rest of the meal. My declaration was unequivocal: 'If we are blessed with children, I will *never* slap them, *ever*'.

While I still do not in any way advocate physical punishment as an effective form of discipline (noting that I discuss this topic in more detail in Chapter Five), at the time, from the lonely, high moral ground of disappointment at my infertility, a parent's choice to shamelessly and openly mete out corporal punishment was just another painful example of injustice. With the benefit of hindsight and the experience of how taxing parenthood actually is, I can be less judgemental of parental actions. The famous saying applies to me: 'Before I had children, I had six good ideas about parenting. Now I have six children and no ideas.'

Acceptance

The journey of acceptance of my infertility was a long one, passing through all the stages of grieving: denial, anger, bargaining and depression before reaching a point where I sort-of accepted it. While I passed through these stages, I was still going through fertility procedures. Truthfully, I hadn't accepted my infertility, even after I adopted. I was still only 38 years old when Kev, my oldest child, came into my life, I was still ovulating, it was still possible that I could get pregnant. What I'm saying is that there was no cut-off point when I said, 'this is it, I've accepted it'. Acceptance was something that grew on me when I eventually settled into my rhythm as a mother.

Is Adoption for Me?

The first mention of adoption sailed over my head, ignored and unprocessed. My concept of motherhood was entirely constituted around the growing of a child in that stubborn womb of mine, of beating the cantankerous system that was preventing me from fulfilling my goal. The eradication of my childless state was about getting a seed to implant in my womb, about experiencing the physicality of swelling with pregnancy, about displaying and showcasing my fecundity, about screaming with the pain of childbirth and being presented with my own flesh and blood within its first moments of life.

The concept of adopting a child had to grow on me first. When Phil mentioned the possibility, I stepped back. Could this work? Could I love unconditionally a child who was not connected to me by blood? A child who had not emerged kicking and screaming from my body after nine months of incubation? As I lay on a hospital bed for one of my (numerous) fertility investigations as a nurse injected dye into my fallopian tubes (*hysterosalpingography), I mulled over the possibility of someone else getting pregnant and giving their child to me.

My experience of adoption was scant. There were no adopted people in either my close or extended family. There were childless relatives, however. A wonderfully handsome uncle and his equally handsome wife were without children. When they visited us from their glamorous, postcard-perfect home in the US, my uncle would repeatedly say to my father as he stared at my three siblings and me: 'You are blessed beyond measure, Malachy.' As a child, I had no idea why my uncle would have thought my father blessed beyond measure, especially as my father would respond by wordlessly shaking his head with his trademark glum expression. The concept that my childless uncle, loaded with money (as enunciated by my father), with a beautiful wife and an abundance of vacations in unimaginable locations such as Florida and Jamaica, could express envy toward my father for the 'blessing' of children was well beyond me.

My limited experience of adoption was via a childless neighbour who had been married some years and out of the blue presented her pink-lipped, creamy-skinned baby to my mother while we were out shopping. While my mother did the usual clucking and oohing over the gorgeous infant, afterwards she uttered the word 'adopted' in a hushed tone, as if the act of adoption was alarming in some way. I enquired why. My mother looked away and muttered something about 'not knowing where the child came from'. I remember trying to reconcile my mother's fearful tone and muttered words with the innocent-faced, pink-lipped baby I had just seen.

I also remember my mother blessing herself when my sister came home from school one day and announced that two of the children in her class were adopted. My childhood perception of adoption was that it was something dubiously mysterious and vaguely shocking, something I didn't quite grasp. In the initial stages of deciding whether to go ahead with adoption, it took some thinking over before I tentatively agreed to complete the first step. In the early weeks of becoming an adoptive mother, joy floating implacably around me, I found myself recalling my early nervousness in considering adoption as a route to parenthood and being seized by shame as a result. How could I have been reluctant to explore any avenue that would bring the miracle of motherhood into my life? How could I have even considered not jumping at the chance? During those heady days of new motherhood, whenever Kev fixed his glorious, unblinking, blue-eyed stare on me, the memory of those initial days of hesitation hit me with an explosion of guilt and recrimination. How could I have even doubted the wonder of adoption? It is said that your first impression is always the most meaningful and accurate. My hesitation was about the lack of blood connection, about not producing a child from inside me. I also realise that my initial reluctance was a natural reflexive reaction to the out-of-syncness that is adoption. It was my instincts at work, my innate realisation that rearing a child who had been tragically separated from his birth parent had to involve loss and sadness for all involved, that my becoming a mother was about someone else giving birth and walking away from their child. I now know that this initial reaction to adoption, like the impression one gets when they meet someone for the first time, has been the driver of my dealings with my children and the driver of my hunger to know whatever there is to know about adoption.

Admitting Infertility

There was another significant aspect to taking that first step in the journey to adoption. By choosing adoption, I was admitting, to myself as much as to anyone, that I was infertile. To adopt was an open statement, a confirmation of the unspeakable: that I was unable to give birth to a child. In making adoption my way of becoming a parent, I was making an open declaration to myself and the world that I wanted to be a mother but was unable to fulfil that want on my own steam. As a prospective mother trying to conceive, I had been plodding along in a miasma of hope (I will surely get pregnant), disappointment (oh no, not another period), expectation (this month it *will* happen), indignation (how could this be happening to me?), tiredness (fertility treatments exhausted me), avoidance (I mostly kept my fertility situation a secret) and at times, devastation. By taking the first step toward adoption, I was admitting my failure in becoming a mother by natural means. I was giving up on becoming pregnant. Even before I took the monumental step of placing our names on a list for adoption assessment, there was readjustment on my part, like bargaining, a process which I now know was a journey toward acceptance, also a recognised stage in the grieving process.

Declaration of Suitability

During the years of waiting to get a 'Declaration of Suitability' to adopt, I mulled over what might be ahead. The whole process of adopting a child took years: there was plenty of time to allow my reservations to increase or lessen. I brooded about holding a child who was not connected to me by blood and what that might be like – whether it would be possible to bond deeply with someone who was not connected by genetics. I reminded myself of the unconditional love I had for Phil, despite the lack of blood connection. We were not related to each other, but that did not thwart the solidity of our bond. I also mulled over the reality of the family system, of the dissension, tension and disrespect that can fester within the cocoon of a family unit. Blood connection frequently fostered enmity and disassociation, the similarity of temperament and inherited traits not always, sadly, ensuring unity, cohesion or loving support. While the majority of families are close, mutually supportive units, many more are shaken by arguments and long-running, stubborn, silence-filled feuds. I comforted myself that blood connection did not guarantee unconditional love and respect. I liked the expression of *Shared Fate*, the title of H. David Kirk's (1984) seminal book on adoptive families. I reached the conclusion that sharing a life created a bond, with or without blood ties. Cheri Register writes: 'I wanted to love a child, to share my life with a child, and hopefully enrich and broaden her life – love her and have her love me' (1991, p. 26). Of course, the desire to give birth did not go away. Even when I sat with a roomful of similarly hopeful-to-adopt couples at various adoption meetings, there was this active 'pregnancy will happen' hope still swimming around inside me. The most positive aspect of taking the first step toward adoption was the opening up of a whole new world. Rather than having my body poked at, I was doing something purposeful, something real, something with a tangible goal at the end.

Pre-Adoption Information Meetings

Prior to the start of the assessment and while my infertility treatment was underway, I discovered the International Adoption Association meetings in the Montrose Hotel, Dublin. What a comfort it was to enter a room where everyone was the same as you. These meetings gave me even greater solace than the National Infertility Support and Information Group, a group I found helpful and affirming due to the general aura of optimism. By attending these meetings and sharing useful information, prospective parents were doing something useful. It was not a support group in the sense of everyone telling their tales of woe – which was fine too – but a network of parents who shared emotionally charged, upbeat adventure stories of hardship and difficult travail to far-flung destinations with happy endings to an enrapt audience.

The Journey to Adoption

At first there was the Health Board assessment. Looking back, it is clear that much of the useful information and situations outlined and discussed during the assessment went over my head due to the dense cloud of infertility angst cluttering my brain. At this point, I was still recovering from the sore of not conceiving. I was a barrel-load of conflicting emotions. Until I fulfilled my desire to parent, my life was at a standstill.

One of the pre-requisites of being assessed for adoption was that the prospective AP had accepted infertility. While this was an appropriate caveat, as being obsessed with the business of getting pregnant would certainly get in the way of digging into the task of preparing for adoption, it was a far from practical one from the point of view of the time constraints involved. The waiting time for assessment was, and still is, anything up to three years. Prospective adopters had already spent a number of years trying for parenthood and if you were to wait until you had accepted infertility (never, maybe?), being too old to adopt was a definite likelihood. In view of the enormity of my desire to parent, it was easy to lie and answer 'yes' to the question of 'have you accepted your infertility?' while the disappointment and insecurity of being an infertile woman rumbled, simmered and smouldered inside me like the witches' cauldron in *Macbeth*.

The assessment consisted of home visits as well as adoptive parenting workshops in the Health Board offices. The latter gave us a chance to be with a group of people who were in the same position as ourselves. Most of the couples we met just wanted to get the whole thing over with, and were, like us, close to burn-out with the assessment red tape and were as unsure about their chosen country.

The visits to our home were the most gruelling aspect of the assessment. I watched the four seasons come and go while we went through the process. The questioning pillaged deep into my heart and challenged every aspect of me. Childhood was examined, financial status, boyfriend history, sex life past and present, religious beliefs, attitude to work, experience of being with children, current domestic environment (e.g., was our house suitable for a child?), plans for childcare and of course, acceptance of infertility. My skin felt as if it was being lifted and looked under.

While I couldn't argue with the intrusiveness – choosing to whom a child is entrusted to is a monumentally responsible job – images of parents who freely and without question produce children they are clearly unable to look after kept coming into my mind. Afterwards, I would chat for hours with my sister and turn over all the questions we had to answer. Theresa would declare that if many biological parents had to go through this assessment to prove suitability to give birth, a large swathe of them would not get through it.

I have many pleasant memories of that assessment time: of long walks around Newbridge with a totally interested and engaged Theresa as I offloaded all my indignation about what I perceived as 'intrusive' assessment meetings. My sister was intrigued by the direction and content of the questioning, particularly about my childhood, which of course was inextricably linked with her childhood. Both of us knew how tense and stormy our lives had been as children. While I answered the social worker's questions truthfully about my childhood (e.g., Q: 'Would you call it a happy childhood?' A: 'Yes, eh, most of the time … you see, we lived in the sticks and were not exactly rich.'), I did not expand on my father's alcohol dependency. My parents had passed away before I got married. By the time I was being assessed for adoption, I had buried my childhood memories and moved on. I saw no point in labouring over family stuff that was over and done with. During the assessment, I kept my positive face to the forefront and focussed on successfully reaching the end of the process.

A Holistic View of Adoption

One thing that really struck me about the adoption assessment back in the late nineties was what I felt to be an air of disapproval from the social workers. While that might well be a projection of my own uncertainty about adoption onto the people to whom I was beholden – I needed the social workers' approval of me in order to adopt – my perception of social workers during that time was of an overriding tone of reproof. However, on reflection, and in the light of all that I have learned about adoption since those heady days when I was under the microscope and my suitability to parent was being judged, I have empathy now for the social workers and their apparent disapproval. Adoption is a complex entity and, as previously mentioned, the joy about to be generated by a couple fulfilling their dream of becoming parents is founded on the sorrow of a birth mother having to relinquish a child. A social worker would have a holistic view of adoption and be equipped to consider the entity from all sides of the triad. As a prospective AP, my opinion was blinkered: I could only see my own need, my own voracious desire to be a parent. After nineteen years of adoptive parenthood, I now understand that any perceived negativity on the part of social workers may have been borne from having been party to and having a greater awareness of, the complexity of adoption.

The Suitability to Parent Document

The preparation for the journey to the depths of Siberia in February 1999 was like a replacement labour, a long litany of painful discomforts – last-minute heart-stopping changes with document dossiers, precarious airplane flights, hair-raising car journeys through packed snow and ice, unpalatable food coupled with nervously empty stomachs, sleepless nights in high-rise apartment blocks and finally, the long walk through the grounds of the grim, grey building called Orphanage Number 2 to where our lives were about to change forever.

From Russia with Love

(Adapted from an article written by me in *Medicine Weekly*, 20 October 1999.)

On a grey February afternoon in 1999, we touched down at a gloomy, dank Domodedovo Airport in Moscow. On first impression, Russia was a sombre place, its citizens' grim-faced and unsmiling. Glum dispositions were not surprising given that barely six months earlier a massive banking collapse had seen customers forming mile-long queues at ATMs in an attempt to retrieve their savings. Economic recession gripped the country.

Our initial task of getting through passport control proved tricky. Phil's passport photo (it was nearly a decade old and he was sporting a beard when it was taken) was scrutinised scrupulously and a number of heavily armed guards took turns gazing sceptically between face and photograph to ensure that they had the correct person. (Afterwards, our interpreter said the extra scrutiny was probably because Phil's bearded visage in his passport photo resembled that of a Chechen rebel.)

With luggage in tow, we battled our way through darkly clad, fur-behatted Russians who crushed tightly around us in the arrivals area. An interpreter called Jana was waiting for us and she introduced us to our driver, Sasha. The airport put-down area was a scene of absolute chaos as cars skidding over slushy, wet pavements blocked each other and frantic beeping took place amongst drivers as they endeavoured to enter and exit.

Our first night was spent with a host family in a high-rise apartment just off Red Square. Sleep eluded us as a pneumatic drill performed road works until 2 a.m. The rest of the night's silence was punctuated by a shrill car alarm that went off intermittently until dawn. The following morning, after breakfast of not particularly appetising bread and ham, we headed for the airport once more to complete the second leg of our journey: a flight across the Ural Mountains to Ekaterinburg, the city where the imperial Romanov family had spent their last days. This was an unforgettable flight. Firstly, Phil barely escaped having his camera confiscated by a security guard as he tried to take a photograph of the ramshackle Ural Airlines aircraft. Then we had a bumpy two-and-a-half-hour flight, luggage on our laps, jam-packed shoulder to shoulder with heavily dressed voyagers, their voluminous coats and fur hats unremoved, the air thick with a melange of body odours, the emergency door clattering on its hinges as we soared across the Ural Mountains.

Upon arrival in Ekaterinburg, we were accommodated by another host family. The following morning, we made the final leg of our journey – 100 miles by car into deepest Siberia. Our party included our coordinator Lena, an interpreter named Anna and a driver named Andre. The countryside through which we drove, our car tyres enshrouded in chains to ensure a grip on the icy surface, was bleaker than bleak. Six feet of packed snow and ice flanked the road. There were miles and miles of uninhabited, snowbound countryside. As we travelled deeper into Siberia we could feel the temperature dropping. It was -13°C when we reached our destination – Nizhny Tagil. While an internet search today reveals a bustling industrial city with its own airport, in February 1999, the place could only be described as cheerless. As we traversed the snow-covered road into the town, residents clad in black from head to toe formed long, disconsolate queues around market stalls.

Our car pulled up outside Orphanage Number 2 and the driver commenced hauling out our bags, which were filled with small gifts for the orphanage staff. The significance of what was about to happen suddenly hit me. I think up to that point I was pulling the old 'head in the sand' routine. I glanced at Phil and knew that his stomach was also churning. On entering the grey spartan building, we were taken endlessly from one Jeyes-Fluid-smelling room to another. I wanted to scream, 'Where is he? Show him to us!' but the set, implacable expressions on the faces around us definitely discouraged such an outburst.

Eventually, after sitting in an office for what seemed like an age but was in reality only about five minutes, we were ushered into a sparsely furnished playroom. The next few moments will be forever etched on my mind. Kev Alexander Vladimir was in a nurse's arms, dressed in a turquoise jumpsuit and green booties. A white woollen hat was pulled over his ears and his face was the colour of white chalk. What a serious, thin, little face it was! I took him in my arms and my first words to him were: 'God, you're so pale!' He stared me straight in the eye, reached over and grabbed a chunk of my cheek in one tiny hand and a chunk of my hair in the other and pulled me in for a closer look. As I kissed both cheeks, he smiled a toothless smile and a pink colour seeped into his face. I was hooked.

A group of nurses hovered around and soon we were told that they would leave the room to allow us to play with him. Phil lifted off Kev's hat and we marvelled at his red hair. As if unseated by the sudden silence and being left alone with two strangers, Kev stretched his legs and we were treated to the first of many ear-piercing squealing sessions. I carried him to the hallway where a huge mirror hung and watched his tears dry as he stared at his own reflection and mine with grave intent. Soon Kev was whisked away by the nurse to be fed and changed for what would be the last time at Orphanage Number 2. We were then presented with a meal. This consisted of what looked like large, greasy, meat-filled pasta shells. Our interpreter and driver dug in immediately. I had to make my apologies and refuse. The reeling events of the morning had rendered my stomach less than sturdy.

Our next task was the court case and a trip to the court house where the judge fired a series of questions in our direction, questions that ranged from whether I intended to go back to work full time to whether we would 'keep the secret of adoption' – the latter to which I answered 'yes', unsure at the time of its meaning and relevance. Eventually, with resounding smacks, she stamped the documents that made Kev Alexander Vladimir our son.

And so, Kev took his leave of the orphanage where he had spent the first eight months of his life. His carer came out to bid him goodbye and gave her name, address and wrote a little message for him. A newly formed family, we bundled into the back of the car for the long return trip and Kev slept in Phil's arms all the way back to Ekaterinburg.

The road from infertility had brought me here, to Siberia, to Kev. The journey, however, was only just beginning.

*Terms mentioned in the chapter:

Hysterosalpingography: X-ray imaging of the uterus and Fallopian tubes following injection of water or a soluble medium.

Intrauterine Insemination (IUI): A procedure for assisting conception in which spermatozoa are injected into the uterus.

Clomifene: A synthetic nonsteroidal compound that induces ovulation.

Human Chorionic Gonadotropin (HCG): A hormone that is produced by the placenta during pregnancy. HCG is given by injection to treat fertility problems.

In Vitro Fertilisation (IVF): Fertilisation of an ovum outside the body with the resultant zygote being implanted in the uterus.

Gamete Intrafallopian Transfer (GIFT): Under laparoscopic or ultrasonic guidance, ova are removed from the ovary, mixed with the partner's spermatozoa and introduced into a Fallopian tube where fertilization takes place.

(Oxford Concise Medical Dictionary, 2007)

Chapter Three

ADOPTION IS COMPLEX

'Adoption is a most difficult and complex process for
everyone concerned.'
Claire Cashin, *Will You Be Here When I Get Home?*

Adoption has three viewpoints: that of the birth mother, the adopted person and the AP. Scrutinizing the three sides of adoption and embracing adoption from the perspective of the two other parties – the birth mother and the adopted child – has provided incomparable learning for this particular AP. Many aspects of what I have learned have saddened me. However, openness to the truth can overcome everything. In researching the writings of birth mothers and adopted people, I grew an understanding of the loss suffered by my children. I then felt equipped (or at least I hope so) to support them in dealing with their grief.

Birth Mother

'The mother who relinquished her child through adoption has long been the forgotten part of the adoption circle. Until recently, it was expected that these mothers would forget about the child whom they had relinquished and that they would continue with their lives as if their child did not exist. For many mothers this was not their experience. They were unable to forget their baby. Ruth J. A. Kelly, *Motherhood Silenced* (2005, p. vii).

'I have counselled so many mothers over the years who are giving up their babies for adoption, and I tell you, Jeanette, they never want to do it. You were wanted – do you understand that?' Social worker to adoptee Jeanette Winterson (2012, p. 185).

'No mother in the world, human or animal, would decide to give up her baby. It isn't natural. It wouldn't happen if mothers had the power to decide. It only happens if they don't.' Barbara Melosh, quoting a birth mother in *Strangers and Kin* (2002, p. 137).

'You don't have someone in your body for nine months and forget.' *Birthmark*, Lorraine Dusky (1979, p. 159).

Understanding how a birth mother might think or feel did not come naturally to me. I had struggled through infertility to become a mother by adoption. The suffering of my child's birth mother was not on my mind.

My most significant insight has been gained through the wonderful writings of two US birth mothers who blog on www.firstmotherforum. com (FMF). When a blog is well written, it is a gift to read. Thanks to the absence of direct editorial influence, pure-gold honesty emerges, truth in all its magnificent beauty. At times, FMF scares me, so direct and unsparing is the tone, so unforgiving of APs, so scathing of adoption. While it is moving to read about birth mothers' suffering and their primal need to reconnect with their lost children, their unabashed hostility throughout the blog toward APs and adoption in general makes for uncomfortable reading at times. However, I believe immersing oneself in writing that comes 'from the horse's mouth' gives a balanced view. How else can one understand adoption, to work through its complexity, than to hear the words of those who took the first step in adoption? Reading this blog has opened my mind to the complexity of adoption. Most importantly, the words of these birth mothers have been a motivator for me in my dealings with my children.

First Mother Forum (FMF)

US journalists Lorraine Dusky and Jane Edwards relinquished their children for adoption in the US in 1966. They explore and document the impact of adoption on the birth mother and adopted person. The blog is also a platform for adopted people and other birth mothers to comment on posts and tell their stories. I will outline a *summary only* (with some direct quotes) and in no particular order of appearance on the blog of the main points made by FMF. The following does contain some candid observations about IA that readers might find upsetting.

- 'Overall, foreign adoption does more harm than good.' The writers believe that APs intentionally try to keep a distance between their adopted child and the child's birth family. 'Some adoptive parents [who] actively seek to adopt from foreign cultures often do so to cut off any real possibility that their children will ever be able to connect with their natural parents.'
- Russian President Vladimir Putin is doing a favour to children by closing down adoptions to Americans. In doing so he is preventing children from being separated from their homeland.
- 'We wonder how the child feels about looking different from everybody around them. We wonder if their parents are really dead, if the child was really abandoned, if she really had been languishing in an orphanage.'
- 'Every parent I know who has adopted from overseas seems to live in a cocoon of self-induced ignorance.'
- 'I hear adoptive parents who say the less they knew (about the birth/first/natural mother) the better, because they did not want to imagine who that other mother was; and when asked, they would be able to honestly say, *I don't know*. But what a terrible loss that is for the [adopted child]. What a terrible thing you have done to him by denying him information about himself.'
- The writers refer to an AP memoir entitled *Baby, We Were Meant for Each Other*. 'When I first got wind of the title a couple of weeks ago, I gagged. It's more of the same that we hear from adoptive parents all the time: this child was "meant" for me, totally subverting the catastrophe in someone's life that led to that child being available to be adopted.'
- 'Adoption is always painful. Or here's a shorter version: "Adoption sucks."'
- FMF applauds APs who make the effort to learn and understand the psychology of adoption as it affects the adopted individual.

Adoption is Complex

On Reading the First Mother Forum

I wanted to exit the page. I felt angry and defensive at the description of APs as 'living in a cocoon of self-induced ignorance', at the blasting of adoption and of IA in particular. I shut my desktop screen, but the FMF's words would not leave my head, the content spinning stubbornly in my brain.

How could I – an AP, and a process into which I had thrown myself wholeheartedly and sincerely – adoption – be the target of such highly charged censure? I reflected on my initial meeting with Kev and all those overwhelming emotions in that frosty children's house in Siberia. Sadness, and even a sliver of shame, ran through me at the 'sickening' description of 'gagging' that was applied to the joy I experienced when I held Kev in my arms for the first time.

Worse still, each claim made in the FMF stung me in a way that insinuated the old adage: 'the truth hurts'. Separation of a child from their birth family has always needled me as a concept. It has always been a part of the adoption process that has sat uncomfortably with me. And here I was reading the words of birth mothers and the first-hand experience of what it was like to relinquish a child.

After I had put aside the initial feelings of anger, guilt and defensiveness, the FMF gave me courage. Birth mothers never forget; birth mothers never recover from giving away their child. The FMF reassured me that trying to make and maintain contact with Kev and Tatiana's birth mothers was not only ethical, but possible and feasible. Talking to my children about their birth mothers allowed them (the birth mothers) to enter into the 'constellation' of us and complete our 'forever' family. The FMF helped me be confident and resolute in my determination to do right by Kev and Tatiana.

A Birth Mother's Grief

One day, Kev (aged thirteen) looked over my shoulder as I was reading Lorraine Dusky's memoir, *Birthmark*. I told him I had just read that birth mothers suffered greatly for having given away their children and it was very likely that (his birth mother) Inna was suffering too. Birth mothers often feel lifelong guilt, sadness and depression as a result of relinquishing their child, something that is not really acknowledged or discussed. Quite resolutely, he declared he wanted to reassure Inna that he was happy and there was no need for her to feel guilty. It was not the answer I expected, and I was relieved and happy that he expressed contentment with his life. However, in the wake of further reading and experience, I realised two important things about what Kev said. Firstly, Kev's grief is separate from his birth mother's grief. While he reassured me that he was happy and wanted his birth mother to know this, it did not remove the presence of his own loss and grief at his relinquishment. Secondly, an adopted person has enough to deal with without having to feel worried about or responsible for their birth mother's guilt and grief. *She* is the one who made the decision, a decision over which they had no control. Therefore, they cannot be expected to rush to console her. If an adopted person feels the need to rush to the support of either their birth mother or AP, then they are not being allowed to acknowledge their own grief, which is specific and individual to them.

The Adopted Person

'I felt different from everyone and believed I didn't fit in the little world where I lived and played . . . I felt alone, so very alone.' Peter F. Dodds (1997, p. 10).

'To be adopted is to be adapted, to be amputated and sewn back together again.' A. M. Homes (2007, p. 20).

AP Nancy Newton Verrier is the author of one of the foremost books in the adoption literature canon. Her seminal book, *The Primal Wound: Understanding the Adopted Child* (1993) was my first piece of adoption reading. Freshly cloaked in the joy of new parenthood, I selected Verrier's book from a recommended reading list in the hope of getting some parenting tips and shared insights. Instead, by the time I got a third of my way through the book, I was weighed down with despondency. What was all this about an infant being forever wounded by the cutting of the biological tie? What was this about a mystical, spiritual connection existing between baby and birth mother, despite separation? Indignation and denial were my strongest emotions. I read as far as Chapter 6 (Abandonment and Loss) before the book got thrown back on the shelf, unfinished.

Adoption is Complex

A decade or more later, I finished *The Primal Wound*. By then I had recognised the issues referred to by Verrier. If there's one thing being an AP has taught me in spades, it is the beauty of honesty. Carl Rogers' words that facts are 'friendly' and that we should not be afraid of what is real applies in adoption like no other situation. I had experienced the grief of my children. I had spoken their birth mothers' names to them and fielded their questions. I had developed enough intuition to see the loss in their eyes, to know that they both experienced the pain of the primal wound as outlined so baldly by Verrier. Once I accepted that separation from the birth mother represents abandonment at its most painful, I was on the road to working through my children's grief.

Being Adopted

'I became the secret keeper of my true feelings, batting inwardly and quietly on the meaning of what it was to be a child who was given up for adoption.' Zara Phillips, *Chosen, Living with Adoption*, (2012, p. 228).

'In adult life, the issue I struggle with most of all is my inadequacy in the presence of others.' Beth Archer, *Chosen, Living with Adoption* (2012, p. 103).

'I am searching for me.' Aoife Curran (2014, p. 174).

'I am neither one thing nor the other. Accepted by neither the British nor recognised by some British-Chinese as being Chinese. I feel like a ghost, invisible to the culture and society that brought me here, but also invisible to the community and culture of my birth.' Lucy Sheen, *Adoptionland* (2014, p. 85).

Adoptees have the least say in the adoption process but are the most affected. Numerous adoptees, as quoted above, volubly express inconsolable anger at the legacy of adoption. Without the courage of adopted people who have written honestly on what it has been like for them, the unresolved issues that imbue adoption would march on, undocumented and hidden. The sharing of experiences by adopted people has been invaluable to me, and for this I express my gratitude. Views of the people most impacted by adoption are vital. How else can APs know or understand? Without their input, everything stays the same and no progress can be made. An adopted child knows one mother abandoned them. It is a burden to grow up with. Non-adoptees could not possibly understand what that feels like. The most common sentence in the adoptee's mind is the question: 'Why was I given up for adoption?'

Nancy Newton Verrier holds the view that *all* adopted people suffer this primal wound as a result of separation from the birth mother. She writes of many adoptees whose adopted status was kept a secret from them; the adoptees demonstrate little or no discernible reaction upon being told of their adoption. This she attributes to an innate knowledge by the adoptee that they were adopted, even though the adoption had been kept secret. She recounts the experiences of adoptees who spoke of never feeling as if they belonged in the family and of not being understood, of not looking like anyone, of not fitting in and not knowing why. One adoptee spoke of discovering in mid-life he was adopted and *not* being shocked at the discovery: he had always felt he didn't fit in with his family. Instead, he felt deeply betrayed by his APs for keeping such significant information from him for all those years. This example alone was enough to illustrate the importance of openness and honesty in all matters surrounding adoption.

APs with whom I've discussed *The Primal Wound* have been critical of Verrier's theory of the primal wound of adoption, declaring that the book was Verrier's subjective experience of adoptive parenthood and that every adoptive relationship is different. A decade after first reading *The Primal Wound*, I happened upon an online thread containing reviews of the book. If I had harboured any doubts about the accuracy of Verrier's claims, the reactions of reviewers (all adopted adults) removed them. Many of the reviewers stated that the existence of a birth family was rarely mentioned while growing up. Acknowledgement of the wound, which they unanimously agreed was primal, was not present during their upbringing. Reviewers expressed concerted congratulations to Verrier for having 'got' them, for understanding and communicating in a unique way what it felt like to be adopted.

Intercountry Adoption (IA)

In the case of IA, the adoptee is required to relinquish heritage and culture as well as their birth family. Not only the blood link, but the opportunity to live amongst people of the same race is severed. In the context of the roughly 5,000 children who were born outside of Ireland and adopted into Ireland, these are the stark, unavoidable aspects of IA. A child is raised in the bosom of a loving home, but there are sacrifices made by that child.

The term 'genealogical bewilderment' is used to describe a sense of disconnectedness, a feeling of being cut off from one's heritage, culture and race. Feeling different from significant people in one's life often has a profound impact on the adoptee's self-concept, writes David Brodzinsky in 1993. Racial diversity adds further complexity to the adoption mix; Brodzinsky writes that physical characteristics help children to define themselves and connect with others. Feelings of belonging and security are nurtured by the similar physical characteristics of the people around you.

Loneliness

Adopted people have written about their feelings of loneliness. They have written of being left out of the 'who looks like who' conversation that dominates most family gatherings; of grandparents who left them out of inheritances in favour of biological offspring; of family friends who asked invasive, unanswerable questions about their birth family. Notwithstanding that loneliness can be experienced by any individual, irrespective of whether they are adopted or not, the AP must be a close, compassionate friend to her child, available whenever needed to compensate for this adoptive loneliness.

Adoptive Parenthood

'Adoptive families navigate emotional terrain that fully biological families don't have to.' Sally Bacchetta (2010, p. xiii).

'We now know, from experience and various studies, that adoptive parenthood requires special qualities.' Rene A. C. Hoksbergen (1997, p. 56).

Adoptive parenthood is laden with both phenomena and miracles: watching your children blossom before your eyes; watching someone so different to you become so like you; experiencing the sadness when you wish, as much as your children do, that they grew in your stomach, that you had carried them for nine months, that you had been the one who had the first glimpse of them; facing the awareness of strangers thousands of miles away, in another country, with faces and personalities resembling the people closest to you, strangers who make up the missing part at the start of your children's lives, a missing part that stays in your consciousness when, as the person closest to them, you can sense your children's loss.

'Blood is thicker than water' is a saying used to describe the tightness of the family bond. This saying infers a substance deficit in non-blood relationships. If the adoption bond is water rather than blood, then water is as much the elixir of life as that red liquid. The water link is coloured with so much love, loyalty, common goals and shared fate, that it turns redder than blood.

Role Handicap

Adoptive father and adoption researcher H. David Kirk, in his seminal 1963 book, *Shared Fate*, describes the conflicts of adoptive parenthood pre-adoption, that is, involuntary childlessness, and post-adoption. According to Kirk, APs experience role handicap, which he defines as: 'A discrepancy between the cultural script and the personal or group encounter with reality' (p. 13). APs rely on the cultural script, which regulates their expectations, the expectation being that they will reproduce a child. The departure (sterility) from the cultural script (fecundity) instigates role handicap: the defined role is now changed.

Society, Kirk writes, is suffused with images of fecundity. APs have little preparation for the spectre of infertility and its impact. The emphasis on fertility revealed in other people's sentiments may dilute the AP's confidence in their own ability. This may, consequently, influence APs to regard their parenthood as less valuable than that of fertile couples with biological children. Kirk writes of APs who express hurt at inappropriate and distasteful remarks that reinforce the sentiment that adoption is second best.

Kirk focuses on the dichotomy of integration versus differentiation. Do we act as if we are the same as any other biological family or do we accept that as a family formed by adoption we are intrinsically different? Kirk refers to one of the dilemmas of role handicap as 'a choice between knowledge and ignorance of the child's forebears' (p. 51). Kirk writes also about two concepts: the 'rejection of difference' and the 'acknowledgement of difference'. These two concepts divide adoptive families into two groups: one family rears children with little or no reference to adoption; the other acknowledges and incorporates adoption into everyday life.

Kirk's 'rejection of difference' concept describes APs who avoid the subject of birth-family history and create a 'pleasant' birth story for their child. Kirk states that such APs face future challenges when the child is old enough to look for a fuller version of the story provided. Kirk's 'acknowledgement of difference' describes APs who take on board their child's birth history and allow their child to grow up with full knowledge of the presence of their birth family.

Post Adoption Depression

'Adoptive parents are expected to be happy to have a child.' Silverstein and Kaplan (1982).

The disappointment, loss and trauma of infertility; the stress of adoption assessment; the uncertainty of the pre-adoption wait; the negotiation of another country's often hostile political and geographical terrain; and the initial explosion of the arrival of a fully formed child all make for an arduous journey into parenthood.

For me, new motherhood was a combination of unbounded joy and fulfilment coupled with anxiety and despondency. Much of postnatal depression is attributed (rightly) to the physical impact on a woman's body of giving birth. The physical hardship of giving birth has not been endured by the adoptive mother. In the eyes of the world, an AP can only feel joy. After all, a long-awaited miracle has arrived and parenthood has been bestowed. I did not feel entitled to declare my low mood as I felt the 'correct' response was gratitude, not grumbling at how desperately tired and anxious I felt. Despite the happiness felt at becoming a mother, I felt exhausted, frustrated and isolated after both fully formed children arrived into my life without the benefit of a nine-month preparation period. In addition to the usual blues felt by any new mother, a host of other anxieties gripped me. In the early days of motherhood, whenever Kev cried, I was convinced that there was something much more serious amiss than hunger, tiredness or a nappy that needed changing. The question 'is this normal or is it because of his adoption?' circulated in my head like unending ticker tape.

Nature or Nurture?

The talents of your adopted child are a reminder of the wonder of nature. You know they did not inherit their singing voice, sporting ability or technical genius from you. You know that you are tuneless, unable to kick a football straight, unable to paint spectacular pictures or effortlessly assemble a power tool. Witnessing their unique talents and individuality is an ongoing wonder for the AP. Not linked by the thickness of blood or the glue of genes, the AP and child are inextricably linked by mutual need and shared history.

Denial of Adoption Grief

'Parents who are in denial of adoptee trauma add another trauma to what the baby's already suffered.' Dr Wendy McCord, quoted in *Twenty Things Adopted Kids Wish Their Adoptive Parents Knew* (1999, p. 51).

At the many wonderfully helpful AP training workshops I have attended over the years, a standard practice has been the enumeration of the challenges of adoptive parenthood as experienced by the attendees. Much like any parenting course, techniques and tips were shared to help APs cope with various challenges. While anger, hoarding, reluctance to share, struggles with writing and reading and excessive temper tantrums were offered by participants as the challenges of adoptive parenting, grief was never mentioned. I could not summon myself to raise my hand and have grief added to the list. Proposing that a child was grieving their adoption and that perhaps the grief was causing anger seemed too controversial and maybe even judgemental. Mentioning grief would also open up a greater Pandora's box, where my own loss at not having given birth would be exposed. The flipside of grief is anger, but naming grief as a component of the adopted child's acting-out behaviour was suggesting a challenge in adoptive parenting that was just too incalculable, too boundless. What could be done about it anyway? The acting out or the struggles with reading and writing were much easier to tackle than examining where that acting-out behaviour might stem from in the first place. Even though I recognised evidence of grief in my children's actions, during parenting courses I was unable to suggest that dealing with grief was one of the challenges of adoptive parenthood. It was safer and more comfortable to remain silent about my grief and their grief. Adoption grief fallout, that is, the adopted child's reactive behaviour that stems from separation from their birth family, is essential to being an AP. It was likely that every AP on that parenting course was aware that all that challenging behaviour was instigated by grief. However, the boundlessness of the topic was a Pandora's box no one was willing or able to open up in the environment of a roomful of strangers, albeit strangers with a common purpose. Sometimes, at these courses, amidst a roomful of APs, I would see an image of adoption grief as a preponderant grey elephant, hunkered down on the floor in the midst of us as we strove to learn how to do the best for our children.

The AP's preservation of silence surrounding adoption grief encapsulates the dichotomy at the heart of adoption. But by sweeping adoption grief under the carpet, APs run a risk. If the loss is air-brushed and the grief swept under the carpet, then the adoptee carries it around with them, unprocessed. Acknowledgment of grief is the key to healing, bonding and progress. Once adoption grief is acknowledged, the grieving person can begin the process of working through the stages of grief. If adoption grief is unacknowledged, then sadness is internalised, unexpressed and subsequently processed into anger, depression and/or anxiety. Acknowledgement of grief eventually leads to acceptance.

Reluctance to talk about grief is explored in a 2016 article by therapist Robyn Gobbel entitled 'Where there is adoption, there is grief'. Gobbel proposes that adoption grief is so big that 'you just can't bear to go there'. She suggests that APs and adoptees 'tell your heart the truth. That you know the grief is there. You aren't ignoring it. You just can't do it right now.'

In referring to adoption, Gobbel writes:

> There are still many, many adoptive families who never disclose to their child that the child is adopted! Really! It's hard to express grief when it's been made so clear that adoption-related grief isn't acceptable. It's not acceptable because there is no problem with adoption. Except there is. There are big problems. Don't get me wrong – there are lots of great things that happen in adoption as well. But we cannot take out of the equation the truth that adoption begins with a tragic loss (2016).

As a culture, we do not tolerate grief well. We expect people to recover from loss within a designated time period without allowances for differences in temperament or varying levels of resilience. And while acknowledgement of adoption grief is the key to healing, grief is a *private* process. The acknowledgement happens privately between parent and child. Beyond the close-knit circle of APs and children, privacy must be preserved.

Disenfranchised Grief

The term 'disenfranchised grief' was introduced by Professor Kenneth Doka, a professor of gerontology, in his 1989 book, *Disenfranchised Grief: Recognizing Hidden Sorrow*. Disenfranchised grief applies where the grief is not generally acknowledged by society. When grief is traditional and acceptable, such as the death of a parent, the griever can be open and expressive. Where the grief is unaccepted and unacknowledged, Professor Doka coined the term 'disenfranchised grief'. Examples of disenfranchised grief include miscarriages or the death of a lover when the affair was a secret. The griever cannot, or at least feels they cannot, openly express their grief. Nobody 'gets' their grief.

Adoption is Complex

Adoption grief falls within this description. Because adoption is seen as the ideal solution, a win-win arrangement, grief is not permitted. The APs 'need' a child and the child 'needs' a parent; it is the perfect symbiotic relationship. However, the whole premise of adoption is founded on loss. Grief permeates adoption from the very beginning when a mother relinquishes her child, to the following step when the AP accepts that giving birth is not going to happen, to the final step when the relinquished child faces a life with a family to which they are not genetically linked.

Reactions to my declaration to specialise in post-adoption loss have confirmed for me that adoption grief is disenfranchised – a grief that is not generally acknowledged or declared. When I announce my intention to specialise in post-adoption support, I am generally greeted with silence. Post-adoption loss is not something that is really discussed.

During an art therapy day, which I undertook as part of my psychotherapy degree, thirty students were seated in a circle and each student was asked to introduce themselves and their career goals. Each student provided information on where they hoped to specialise – some hoped to work with children, some with rape victims, some with the suicidally bereaved and so on. After each student had introduced themselves, the tutor made a comment on their plans, offering some tips on how to obtain further training and wishing them luck. When it came to my turn, I stated my intention to train as an adoption professional to help with adoption grief and loss. The tutor stared at me for a few moments, and without as much as a comment, moved on to the next student. While I was embarrassed at being blanked by her in front of thirty people, I was aware that I was experiencing the impact of silence in relation to the acknowledgement of adoption grief.

On another occasion, when I was chatting with an adoptive mother at a school event, I said I was pursuing a degree in psychotherapy and hoped to specialise as a post adoption professional. She misunderstood and thought I was intended to set up an agency to facilitate adoptions for couples hoping to adopt and commented that she had also considered doing the same thing. When I explained my actual career goal – to help those touched by adoption loss and grief – the adoptive mother looked away, spotted another friend, wished me luck and walked off. The wordless response seemed to imply: 'Why are you even talking about this?'

Evelyn B. Robinson, who relinquished her child for adoption, writes in *Adoption and Loss – The Hidden Grief* that 'Adopted people often raise issues of their sense of identity and sense of belonging. Because they are told that, by virtue of being adopted, they are "special", "chosen" and "fortunate", their grief at the separation from their natural mother is denied, by society and often by their adoptive parents' (2003, p. 155). The adoptee is considered by society to be 'lucky' because they have been taken in by a family and saved from the life of an orphan. They have been taken out of economic deprivation and 'saved' by their adoptive family. Clare Cashin writes: 'The most frequently used defence against painful feelings and methods of self-protection can be easily observed in an adopted person's denial and avoidance of these feelings' (2006, p. 52).

There is an understandable fear in having an open discussion about adoption grief, as the discussion stokes potentially complex family issues. Privacy is essential in relation to the tracing and identifying of the birth family of the adoptee. There is, however, a subtle difference between open discussion and privacy. In a general acknowledgement and open discussion of adoption grief, the bottling-up can come to an end. The open discussion takes place in a private setting where the griever can express their feelings and release pent-up sadness. The saying 'if you name it you can tame it' coined by Marc Brackett accurately describes the process.

Acknowledgement

Adopted persons will say that the *acknowledgement* of their grief by their adoptive family would have been enough; even a discussion about their birth history, however cursory, would have helped, or just something to affirm the feeling of loss. Often, all we need is someone to say they understand why we feel the way we do, to confirm that we are not off the wall because we feel empty or deprived. Such is the case with the adopted person.

Peter Dodds writes of the denial of his adoption grief by his APs. When he was told he was adopted and the tears came, his father asked 'Why are you crying, Peter? Be Strong. Big boys don't cry' (1997, p. 3). Dodds described the emotions he experienced as he grew up: 'Grief, sorrow, helplessness, guilt, fear, embarrassment, rage, rejection, anger, shame, inferiority' (p. 5). He writes of 'being uprooted, of not belonging and being different' (p. 13). He accuses his APs of taking him away from 'the land of his birth, blood, language and heritage' (p. 13).

The importance of openness is summarised in a novel called *The Adoption* by Ann Berry: 'Better to know and drop down into the bubbling cauldron, than live with question marks' (2012, p. 86). Acknowledgement of the grief and loss in adoption is the greatest gift we can give ourselves and our adopted children.

The Expression of Grief

The stages of grief as per Elizabeth Kubler Ross are: denial, anger, bargaining, depression and acceptance. I have witnessed these stages – not in any order – in my children as they have moved toward adulthood. Anger was common, depression also, denial too. When displays of grieving occurred, I would remind myself that a child whose biological parent walked away from them could only be working through grief. I accepted their expressions of grief as part of who they were. When challenged with angry, over-the-top outbursts and stubborn opposition, I had to be aware not to trounce on thinly veneered insecurity – a skill acquired with much difficulty and after many mistakes! (Note: this awareness did not stop me from being mad as hell or from, on far too many occasions, roaring my head off at them! However, it did keep me focused in understanding where it was coming from.)

Nancy Newton Verrier writes of control as a 'foil to loss' and that one of the ways in which children try to prevent future losses is to attempt to be in control of every situation. Verrier writes that the simplest household decision or suggested deviation from routine can become an immense struggle for control. It isn't just a matter of opinions or taste, she says, it is a matter of survival. The child was not in control of the situation at the beginning of their life and look what happened.

When Tatiana was twelve years old, I found a poem written by her on my phone. Her words encompass the complexity of emotions of any child on the brink of adolescence, but particularly an adopted pre-adolescent.

A Note of What It Feels Like to be Me

I scream for help
But there is no reply.
I suffer in pain
But there is no cure.

I make mistakes
But there is no correction if it's
Right or wrong.
I try to fit in
But I am invisible to everyone.

I try to do the right thing
But when I do the right thing
You're not there.

Grief must be accepted by APs as the child's understandable reaction to relinquishment and separation at birth. In accepting that grieving is inevitable, we can help our children before their behaviour turns into an illness for which medical or psychological treatment is necessary. Anticipating grief-related acting-out behaviour and dealing with it in an empathic way will allow our children to move through the stages of grief, toward acceptance and the achievement of post-traumatic growth.

Getting Help with Adoption Grief

'Go on, throw me into the rubbish heap.' The words of a nine-year-old adopted child reflecting on being relinquished by her birth parents (as shared by the AP).

Once you have accepted that your child is grieving, what next? While there are many behavioural experts available with suggested techniques to help you parent a child who is challenging, finding someone with expertise in helping with the specifics of adoption grief requires careful research by the AP. The last thing you want to do is introduce your grieving child to a so-called expert who is dismissive or ignorant of the impact of the primal wound. It is essential to enlist the services of someone who can be trusted to understand the delicate, sensitive and very individual nuances of adoption (See Useful Services).

Often the child has reached adolescence before therapy is sought. For any child, whether adopted or with their biological family, teenage years bring up an amalgam of emotions and questions. Being a teen is a complex business anyway; being adopted adds a further challenge.

In *Beneath the Mask: Understanding Adopted Teens* (Riley and Meeks, 2006), Dr Joyce Maguire Pavao writes of the dangers of professionals labelling adopted children with 'whatever the current designer diagnosis is'. Riley and Meeks also refer to the paucity of adoption experience amongst therapists: 'My heart breaks when families and teens come in and reveal that they have seen multiple therapists who never asked about adoption or seemed comfortable talking about it' (p. xxii).

Another key aspect to be aware of is the tendency of clinicians to diagnose a grieving child as having ADHD, as the child's behaviour displays similar characteristics to this disorder. Many APs have reported that after a short consultation (less than ten minutes in one case), the child was diagnosed with ADHD and a prescription for Ritalin given. Needless to say, giving Ritalin to a child who needs to express their grief is a shortcut to disaster.

In *Chosen: Living with Adoption* (2012), Frankie Pearse wrote how her therapist couldn't accept that she wanted to talk about her birth mother all the time. Pearse advises that 'if you decide to go for counselling make sure you go to someone who specialises in adoption or fostering' (p. 53).

Betty Lifton, adoptee and author of *Lost and Found: The Adoption Experience*, writes in a 2010 article of what she described as 'ghosts' in the adoption relationship. For a therapist to help adoptees and their APs, the therapist must be able to see the ghosts that accompany them. These ghosts spring from the depths of unresolved grief and trauma that both parties have experienced: loss of potential biological children by the APs and the loss of birth parents by the adoptee. Professionals cannot really see the adoptees and APs that enter the therapy room unless they can see the ghosts that accompany them.

Sometimes Love Is Not Enough

Despite the primal desire that first sends a prospective parent down the adoption route, adoptive parenting is not without its well-publicised failures. The many contradictions and conflicts inherent in adoption often manifest in tragedies that reveal and illustrate adoption's darker side. Any internet search will display a plethora of adoption tragedies: children who have been abused by their APs, who have been sent back alone to their country of origin, who have been returned to institutional care, or, the most horrifically tragic of all – who have been allegedly killed by their APs.

Lack of appropriate preparation by APs is a key component in such appalling tragedies. The long road to adoption is a test of any prospective AP's determination and desire. Preparation must include perusal of the impact of combined traumas of time spent in institutional care and separation from the birth parent. The unprepared, unsuspecting AP, without the availability of appropriately skilled post-adoption support, faces the stress of parenting a victim of early childhood trauma.

In the pre-adoption stages, adoption can be sugar-coated. All parties are portraying their best side – prospective APs want to become parents and health authorities want to see a child placed with a family. In order for adoption to be successful, emphasis needs to be placed as heavily on post-adoption support as ensuring, pre-adoption, that the AP is suitable to parent.

The news in 2010 that an adoptive mother sent her seven-year-old child back to Russia induced a sharp intake of collective breath from adoptive families worldwide. Artyom Saveliev's pale, handsome little face beamed out from photos circulated worldwide and vilification of his AP, Torry Ann Hansen, reached hysterical proportions. Much of the vilification came from prospective APs, as shortly afterwards Russia suspended adoptions to the US. See the April 2010 issue of a *New York Times* article by Damien Cave. At age six, Artyom was removed from the care of his birth mother who was an alcoholic. At age seven, he was adopted by Torry Ann Hansen. Artem had spent the first six years of his life in the care of an alcoholic parent and then removed from his home to a children's institution. He was then adopted by a woman from another culture (Hansen), moved to new surroundings in the midst of strangers, learned to speak a foreign language, had his name changed, ate strange food and learned to fit in with people who were strangers to him. The chaos within his short life was obvious. As well as early childhood trauma as a consequence of traumatic parenting and a period of time in institutional care, Artyom endured the displacement of intercountry adoption as insightfully described by AP Cheri Register: 'Intercountry adoption is not ideal or trouble-free. Being separated from family and displaced at a tender age to a foreign culture, where sights, sounds, smells, [and] tastes are vastly different, is an abnormal circumstance' (2005, p. 37).

This child was separated from his birth parent, albeit a parent who was an alcoholic. Separation from the mother he had known for most of his life equated to bereavement. After a stint in an institution, Artem was given a chance at a better life, but this chance involved displacement to a foreign culture. It's not hard to imagine how seven-year-old Artem might be angry and chaotic in a way that his adoptive mother interpreted as 'violent and psychopathic' – attachment issues alone would dictate such behaviour, not to mention the confusion and anxiety generated by landing in a completely strange environment – abnormal circumstances indeed.

Equally, it's not hard to see how the AP, Torry-Ann, was desperately at sea with how to rear her new child and why she might have interpreted his exhibition of trauma as evidence of 'severe psychopathic issues'. Early childhood trauma and its impact on a child's behaviour has the potential to beat even the most resilient of APs. Interacting empathically in an attachment-parenting way (as outlined in Chapter Six) with a traumatised child is a start. However, this is a technique that the AP must be provided with and then educated on.

Support from adoption professionals who understand the impact on a child of parental abandonment, institutionalisation and the role of attachment in adoption would certainly have ensured Artyom made strides in settling into his new family. As an AP, I am aware that lavishing love on a child is not enough. Understanding the child's attachment issues and the impact of their grief, combined with a mammoth dollop of patience and self-care, are essential elements of adoptive parenting. By definition, adoption forms a legal bond where the adopted child is, to the AP, the same as if 'born to them in wedlock'. Therefore, the concept of 'giving a child back' cannot apply. A family cannot 'give back' a child born to them – she/he is permanently their child. Adoption is the same. When entering into an adoption agreement, the APs accept that the child is theirs for life, for better or for worse. (In the spirit of an adoption being permanent, Torry Ann Hansen was subsequently ordered by the courts to pay child maintenance for Artyom, the child she sent back to Russia.)

If the child needs help, then the onus is on the family and health authorities to obtain that help. The reality is that the assessment does not objectively examine the likelihood of struggles for APs post adoption. When the assessing social worker mentions (during pre-adoption assessment) possible behaviours as a result of abandonment and institutionalisation, the reflex reaction of the prospective parent is denial, as they are still 'under scrutiny' and trying to prove they are suitable to adopt; I should know, as I was in that position myself!

Pre-adoption, the prospective parent is full of hope, optimism and ignorance while the health authority is looking for the best possible home for the child. Neither party has the capabilities to discuss what comes after, because it is unknown. While it is obviously essential that the parents are properly assessed for suitability, it is even more essential that when the child is at home with their new parents, appropriate supports are automatically put in place, supports that can be accessed without the barrier of the AP's shame (am I failing as a parent?) or self-flagellation.

If appropriate post-adoption support had been made available to the APs of disrupted adoptions, the children would have had a greater chance of remaining with the adoptive family. Of course, there are exceptions to any rule, but with appropriate help and support available, I believe preservation of the family is possible and essential.

Getting Support – Personal Experience

My experience of receiving help occurred when Tatiana was nine years old and spoke of her sadness when she thought of her birth family. Thanks to the wonderful support provided by the Barnardos Post Adoption Service (much gratitude to Andrew Walker), Tatiana was able to process her grief. One of the most effective methods Andrew used to help Tatiana was a 'parts' exercise, in which Tatiana lay on a large sheet of paper on the floor and I drew an outline of her. Throughout this drawn outline she wrote lists of all the other aspects of herself besides her adoption: her adoptive family, her friends, her talents and gifts, her favourite school subjects, hobbies, television programmes, movies and movie characters, novels, music, pets and holiday destinations. She was simply creating a snapshot of all aspects of her as a person, not just defined by one aspect (her adoption), but rather several aspects which constituted the individual that she was.

Conclusion

'The joy and the tragedy co-exist. That is the paradox of adoption.' Cheri Register (2005, p. 11).

Acknowledgment by the AP of the complexity of adoption, together with an open approach to allowing full expression of grief, is an important step on the road to healing for both the AP and the adopted child.

Chapter Four

THE THINGS PEOPLE SAY

'People who have had no intimate contact with adoption and
its meanings may unintentionally add to the burden of the
adopters' role handicap by remarks and questions that set
adopters and their children apart.'

H. David Kirk, *Shared Fate*

Dealing with the things people say can be a testing aspect of adoptive parenthood, particularly in the early days. Cheri Register writes: 'The questions and comments betray ignorance about how adoption works and the day-to-day experience of adoptive families, not to mention the insensitivity to the children themselves. We don't get negative comments, but we sure hear a lot of dumb things' (1994, p. 104). H. David Kirk outlines in *Shared Fate* the sense of alienation experienced by many APs due to the remarks made by others, remarks that infer that adoption is inferior to biologically reproducing as a means of forming a family.

People who come into contact with newly adopted children and their parents often suffer from massive foot-in-mouth disease. The absence of the standard chit-chat about who the child looks like renders a void in the conversation. The void is often filled by various well-meaning but insensitive comments, many of which have totally confounded me. I hope this chapter will help in a two-fold way. Firstly, it might encourage non-adopters to think and reflect before emitting patronising and tactless comments and secondly, to support APs in developing a language to field those same comments with dignity, grace and confidence.

I didn't respond to most of the comments that came my way. Instead, I just walked away, inwardly seething – not a good thing for my general well-being – but at least placing distance between me and the speaker. But I did keep a mental note of all of the comments and questions I encountered as well as similar experiences other APs have shared with me. I want to emphasise that not all of the things said to me were negative; some things made me laugh out loud. Most of the comments showed ignorance, which is understandable in the light of the absence of available information on adoption's intricacies and nuances, and others showed that they were just ignorant of the complexities of adoption. I hope that by sharing, APs will realise they are not alone and that my suggestions for suitable responses might help. Also, it might encourage non-adopters to pause for thought before making what could be an insensitive, hurtful remark.

I also know that the following will be deemed by some as being over-sensitive. But, heck, I don't care! They're my feelings and I'm owning them.

The Impact of Words

'Be impeccable with your word. Speak with integrity. Use the power of your word in the direction of truth and love.' Don Miguel Ruiz, *The Four Agreements* (1997).

At the many AP training workshops I attended, irrespective of the theme of the workshop, the impact of the comments made by other people to adoptive families invariably featured. Intrusive questions, callous statements (some quite racist) – were described by APs. This aspect of adoptive parenting has taught me a valuable lesson for other aspects of my life. What you say can have a huge impact, irrespective of who you are. Therefore, it is of major importance to think before you speak, no matter who you are talking to. As quoted above by Ruiz, the importance of being impeccable with your word cannot be overstated.

Since becoming an AP, I've learned that there are lots of things that are difficult to say, the most difficult being beginning the adoption conversation with your child. Equally, I now know too well just how easy it is for other people to make statements about adoption without realising the potential hurt being caused.

An AP once said you become public property when you adopt a child, as if the manner in which you became a mother bestows a *carte blanche* to all and sundry to ask insensitive questions which, if directed toward biological parents, would be regarded as a serious faux pas.

Family Can Be the Worst

Family can often cause the most hurt; the fact that they are family and supposedly in our corner increases the impact of the hurt. The most cutting barbs are often from those closest to us. The extended family often struggles with being excluded from the previous history of the child who is in their midst (the adopted child) and consequently are unsure of whether or not to ask questions about the child's history; if they do ask questions they are often unable to deal with being told that the child's birth information is not available for discussion with them.

This is one of the many complexities of adoption – the existence of another family, separate and distinct from the adoptive family and *private* to the child – privacy being the key word. The child owns the exclusive rights to the discussion of their birth family. APs rightly keep their child's history within the 'golden circle' of themselves and their child – a close family unit. If the child wishes to share their birth information at a future date, then that is their exclusive right. One adoptive father described a scenario at a family wedding where he overheard a female acquaintance loudly asking a question in relation to his daughter: 'Who is her mother?' (meaning: 'Who is her *birth* mother?') His mother-in-law, to whom the question was posed, answered within the adoptive father's earshot, in what he described as a strident, conspiratorial tone: 'We don't know. We haven't been told'. The adoptive father described his hurt and anger at his mother-in-law's tone and response as well as the inappropriateness of the enquiry by the acquaintance. The question 'Who is her mother?' exemplified the lack of understanding of the sensitivities of adoption. The tone and wording of 'We haven't been told' illustrated the sense of entitlement to personal information. A more fitting response to the churlish question might have been: 'That's something we can only talk to the child herself about whenever she is ready,' or 'That's private, between my son and his family', followed by a swift change of subject.

Avoiding Potential Hurt – Role Handicap

In the early years of adoptive parenthood, if I suspected a social situation could bring me into the company of people who would potentially make offensive comments, I avoided the situation. Being a thin-skinned person, I have consciously avoided people or situations where comments were likely to be made. I realise now that this was all part of the 'role handicap' I suffered as an AP, as described by Kirk in *Shared Fate* – my role was not the expected one of fertility (giving birth) but was instead one of sterility (adoption).

Telling my 'Giving Birth' Story

Giving birth has to be one of life's greatest experiences. I have no doubt that if I had gone through it, I would probably want to talk about it a lot. However, in the early days of adoptive motherhood, when birth stories were recounted in my presence, role handicap prevented me from being open and expansive about my adoptive parenthood. While attending a fundraiser for Kev's primary school, I was standing in a circle with some mothers to whom I had recently been introduced. One woman began talking about giving birth. 'I had twenty hours of it. It was like someone was trying to open up an umbrella inside me.' The woman beside her made her contribution: 'I was dilated for hours – it was a fierce dash to the hospital'. The next woman spoke of the painful stitching that had to be endured. Another spoke of inflamed nipples. Anecdotes of pain and wounds moved around the arc of the circle like a rapidly spreading bush fire and veered unstoppably towards me. Soon it would be my turn to contribute to a group of people whom I barely knew and who were unaware of my adoptive status. The anticipation of their reaction to my announcement of adoptive parenthood made me beyond uncomfortable. I was not in the mood for the standard, patron-ising chorus of: 'Well, aren't you wonderful?' reserved for us so-called 'brave and altruistic' APs. I looked around the hall in panic and with the utmost gratitude spotted another mother I recognised. I stepped away from the group just as it was my turn to speak, made a big show of greeting the newcomer loudly and brought her into the circle of mothers. The wildfire stopped. Potential embarrassment was averted. I should of course be oblivious to the comments of others and be loud and proud in proclaiming my AP status, but early on in motherhood, my role handicap restricted me, and my sensitivity took over.

Intrusive Questions

On another occasion, I was interrogated by a male guest whom I had never met before while attending a family wedding. He asked me what medical condition I had that caused me to adopt a child. 'Why did you have to adopt?' the man unabashedly asked. Despite my obvious discomfort, this stranger doggedly pursued his line of questioning, enquiring as to whether I had had medical investigations! I still remember walking away in a fury after mumbling some answer. Such rude intrusiveness made me happy to avoid large family gatherings, at least while my adoptive parenthood was in the early stages and I was settling into my role. As my children grew older and were more established in my life, those questions seemed to lessen – or maybe I just wasn't invited to many family gatherings – who knows!

Barbara Melosh writes:

> Probing questions posed to **biological** parents are widely recognised as rude and intrusive; few ask, 'Was it a mistake, or did you plan this pregnancy?' 'This baby doesn't look like your husband, are you sure he is the father?' Adoptive families, by contrast, are routinely subject to intrusive questions. 'Are those kids yours?' is a frequent query posed to adopters in 'non-matching' families. APs are often asked, sometimes in earshot of their children, 'Why was he put up for adoption?' or 'Who are his real parents?' 'What did it cost?' Congratulations to new adopters are often offered along with the comment, 'Maybe you'll still have a child of your own' (2002, p. 286).

The Things People Said:

That Made Me Laugh

Des, a tradesman, was in a neighbour's house and I was chatting with Des and my neighbours about a painting job I needed to get done. Kev was in my arms, aged about thirteen months. Des did not know

Kev was adopted. Kev began to get restless and started to whinge, interrupting the flow of the chat. While I was trying to soothe him, Des said: 'Oh, you'll have to send him back'. Des, unaware I was an AP, was merely making a facetious comment about Kev's whinging. However, the smiling expressions on my two neighbours' faces changed immediately to alarm as they both knew I had just adopted Kev. They both stared at me in abject horror at Des's comment and awaited my response. It was their shocked expressions at Des's careless utterance that amused me the most. I knew he did not realise he was talking about an adopted child and his declaration of punishing the child for crying by 'sending him back' was just a throwaway one that I've heard older people use. There was no malice intended and none taken. My neighbours continued to stare at me wide-eyed in a stunned silence until I brushed it away by hugging Kev, saying 'I couldn't do that', and continued to talk about the painting job.

I once met a former schoolmate who didn't know I was a parent by adoption. He stated that Kev bore a great likeness to my biological family; he was 'cut out' of my cousins and 'spat out' of my uncle. I had fun with this one: 'Not unless my uncle was having great fun out in the wilds of Siberia,' I answered, as I explained to him that I had adopted Kev.

That Made Me Cringe

'Aren't you brave?' This usually comes from women who have given birth. The inference is that anyone who adopts needs more courage than someone who goes through the nine months of pregnancy and then yields themselves up to the often risky, physical trauma of childbirth. I replied: 'Giving birth is no picnic either, you were brave to have gone through it all three times. Well done you!' I've never actually asked them to spell out what exactly they thought was brave, as it seemed too confrontational and I didn't want to have to listen to their attempts at giving examples of my braveness.

'You will have a couple of children of your own now'. The inference of this statement is that (a) now that I have attained motherhood status, I will relax, and it will all happen naturally and (b) the adopted child is not really my own and giving birth is a much better option. My reply to that one is usually: 'I have my own child now.'

'Which child is your own?' This question was posed by an acquaintance to a mother standing with her three children, one biological and two adopted. All three children heard the question and three pairs of eyes were trained on the mother as she, without hesitation, responded: 'All three are my own'.

'He's a very lucky boy'. The inference here being that the child would be in the gutter if it wasn't for you, the generous AP, and that he should be eternally grateful for being adopted by someone as wonderful as you. The response to that nugget, which was bestowed upon me by several older members of my extended family, was simply: 'It is we who are lucky'.

That Made Me Sigh and Say Nothing

'He looks very normal'. I didn't respond to this snippet of wisdom delivered by a neighbour as a 'welcome to the neighbourhood' greeting for Kev, but really felt like asking 'What is normal?'

'Why should he feel any sadness, sure he knows you chose him?' I had been talking about adoption grief and how it was normal for it to go hand-in-hand with adoption, and this was the response. The person was trying to comfort me by giving me a way to comfort my child, that is, telling him he was chosen. All I could do was sigh and be reminded again how adoption is so misunderstood. The child naturally feels sadness, and an AP telling a child they were chosen above others does not in any way assuage that sadness.

'Adoption is a great facility for infertile couples, isn't it?' This came from a fertile mother and showed a profound lack of understanding of the actuality of adoption. When she used the word 'facility' to praise adoption, I felt ice in my stomach.

Comments Shared by Other APs

'Thank God he doesn't have those funny eyes the Russians have'. An AP's acquaintance said this with relief in her voice. Needless to say, not much contact was made from then on with that acquaintance.

'Where did you import him from?' An AP received this enquiry from a casual acquaintance when the AP took his newly adopted son shopping for the first time. The choice of words rendered the child to the status of a commodity and revealed deep insensitivity on the part of the speaker.

'You are adopting from Russia – sure they're all thieves and murderers out there.' A close family member of an AP declared this when they announced their plans. This statement revealed volumes about the speaker and their ability to dismiss a whole nation in one throwaway comment.

W.I.S.E. Up

I discovered the W.I.S.E. Up programme, which helps adoptive families deal with intrusive questions and comments, when I was already a number of years into adoptive parenthood. The programme was developed in 1998 by the Centre for Adoption Support and Education (C.A.S.E.) in Maryland, US. C.A.S.E. is a mental health service located throughout the US that provides professional support to adoptive and foster families. W.I.S.E is an acronym for: Walk away, Ignore or change the subject, Share what you are comfortable sharing, and Educate about adoption in general. The W.IS.E. Up programme is based on the premise that adopted children are wiser about adoption than peers who aren't adopted. Walking away and ignoring or changing the subject were my own ways of dealing with unwanted enquiries. Sharing and educating followed later when I was more settled into my role.

Conclusion

The absence of discussion and widely available literature about the complexities of adoption is likely one of the reasons why people give unhelpful comments to adoptive families – people who don't understand adoption are unsure of what to say. While most comments are made in good faith and reveal ignorance rather than negativity toward adoption, equally the complexity of adoption lends itself to many a hurtful and unforgettable statement. The W.I.S.E. Up programme is to be recommended as a way of coping with unwanted statements.

On an optimistic note, things do get better – having reared my two children to adolescence and beyond, tactless comments are less frequent – certainly one of the many gifts of growing older.

Chapter Five

The Wonder of Self-Evaluation

'The best thing you can do to help your child is to grieve
your own losses which may have occurred prior to adoption
– losses such as infertility, miscarriage, stillbirth or death –
and to let yourself feel sad for your child's losses and your
inability to protect him from whatever happened to him
prior to joining your family. Only then can your adopted
child's losses be validated and then grieved together in an
atmosphere of openness and honesty.'

Sherrie Eldridge, *Twenty Things Adopted Kids
Wish Their Adoptive Parents Knew*

Self-evaluation helped me understand my feelings about the complexity
of adoption: the loss of the biological connection, both mine and
theirs; the reality of my children being born to someone else; and my
children's grief at their loss of a biological connection. We are ready to
talk about adoption to our child when we have accepted its complexity.

All children, adopted or with their biological parents, are 'borrowed'
to some extent. Every child is an independent entity, only in our care
until they are ready to take flight. The challenge of adoptive parenthood is the acceptance of the child having their own separate family,
unfamiliar to us. The existence of another family can destabilise an
AP's confidence by diluting the strength of their right to parenthood.
The presence of another woman – the birth mother – reminds us what
wasn't achieved – we did not give birth, and another woman is the
bearer of our precious child. This perception of a dilution of the right
to parenthood and consequent loss of confidence as a parent impacts
on the relationship between AP and child.

The Wonder of Self-Evaluation

When the reality of the complexity of adoption is accepted by the AP, their confidence as a parent increases. Therefore, an essential aspect of strengthening an AP's confidence is to acknowledge and accept the complexity of adoption: the existence of another set of parents in the relationship; the reality that you, the AP, were not there at the crucial opening days, weeks, months or years of your child's life; that before you came into your child's life, there was someone else, someone genetically closer than you, someone blood-linked to your child, someone your child will grieve for no matter how much you strive for excellence as a parent. Self-evaluation will help us grieve our own losses and in turn, our children will benefit. In this section I will suggest some ways to self-evaluate, beginning with the official 'examination' of prospective parents: the adoption assessment.

The Adoption Assessment – Examining Suitability to Parent

Prospective APs are obliged to undergo an adoption assessment of suitability by the HSE. The assessment evaluates suitability for adoptive parenthood as well as offering AP training. H. David Kirk (1984) wrote that one of the most difficult aspects of adoption was having to depend on the assistance of outsiders (such as an agency) to become a parent.

Prospective APs know they have to prove themselves during assessment. There's little room for doubt or negativity. Similar to a job interview, you minimise your shortcomings and focus on your strengths. While any prospective parent, biological or adoptive, can be apprehensive about child rearing, any apprehensions held by the prospective AP are unlikely to be aired during the assessment for fear of not being passed fit to adopt. Everything is positive and upbeat: best foot forward at all times!

You talk about your childhood (all the sunny parts), tell them your family are thrilled with the idea of you adopting a child, assure them that you have accepted your infertility and have ceased all fertility treatments. Again, like a job interview, you present yourself in the best possible light in order to get the job. Even if the assessing social worker was to refer to possible post-adoption challenges, such as potential issues resulting from time spent by your (prospective) child in institutional care, your defensive antennae are fully erect. So grateful are you for a chance to become a parent that your mantra, espoused with absolute conviction, is: 'I am confident I will cope with *anything.*'

Here are some adoption-assessment questions:

> Why do you want to become parents?
> What does having a child mean to you?
> What experience do you have with children?
> Have you spent time minding children?
> Are you familiar with caring for a baby?
> How will you cope with being woken up during the night?
> How would you cope if your child develops a disability?
> What kind of childcare will you use if both parents continue to work outside the home?
> How will you discipline your child?

The assessment is suitably thorough – it is, after all, about ensuring a child is placed within the best possible family. However, at times, it does border on intrusive. For instance, our social worker asked me if I enjoyed my first sexual experience. Apart from the cringing embarrassment of outlining such information to a stranger with my husband sitting on the sofa beside me, the question stood out in its inanity. How could a person's first attempt at sexual intercourse impact on suitability for parenthood? When challenged on the pertinence of the question, our social worker immediately backed down and moved on to the next section.

While in the throes of the assessment, it occurred to me more than once that if *every* prospective parent, not just adoptive, had to go through such an inquisition before bringing a child into the world, fewer children would be neglected or forced to endure a childhood of feeling unwanted and rejected. Being assessed for your suitability to parent forces you to *really* think about what being a parent is about.

How to Self-Evaluate in Three Steps

Self-evaluation involves looking into our past and reflecting on the events of our childhood that shaped us as people and ultimately as parents. All of us carry baggage from our childhoods; it is nigh impossible to have reached adulthood without having had trials sent our way. The image of an idyllic childhood is just that – an image. How we have dealt with our personal trials is the key issue, and becoming a parent excavates buried material like no other. The mix of parental responsibility, passionate love, commitment and guilt produces a cauldron that bubbles and boils within us. It hangs over all of our interactions with our growing child. Our child being adopted adds an extra ingredient to the mix – the complexity of adoption.

Jana Wolff writes:

> The process of adopting a child pushes your personal envelope as a woman, as a mother, and ultimately, as a human being. It takes more courage than you think you have, offers more self-knowledge than you think you have, offers more self-knowledge than you think you want, and reassembles your characteristics into someone familiar but changed (2010, p.19).

Examining how I was parented helped me see how my own parenting style was developed, which in turn helped me accept the complexities inherent in adoption. Hughes and Baylin write: 'While living with your parents as their child, you were learning how to be the parent of your child' (2014, p. 214).

Step One – Three Books to Read

1. *The Drama of Being a Child* by Alice Miller

A perusal of Alice Miller's classic 1987 book is the first step on the road to self-examination. Any parent (biological or adoptive) would benefit from reading Miller's brutally frank book, which examines the consequences of physical and psychological harm done to children and its cost to society. This is a short book, fewer than 40,000 words, but is substantial in content and message – this book really strikes a chord. I was initially unimpressed with Miller's bold, sweeping statements about parenting, especially when she wrote that 'every childhood's traumatic experiences remain hidden and locked in darkness' (p. 5) and of adults who 'suddenly get the feeling they have failed to live up to some ideal image or have measured up to some standard' (p. 6). I was uncomfortable and irritated and wanted to post a review contradicting Miller's many positive ones. I wanted to open the review as follows: 'Alice Miller is talking through her a**e.'

But it was her *truth* that made me uncomfortable and irritated, not any perceived inaccuracies or sweeping statements. That I was reacting so vehemently to her words was proof that she had hit a nerve. Miller writes: 'Most people [...] continue to live in their repressed childhood situation, ignoring the fact that it no longer exists. They are continuing to fear and avoid dangers that, although once real, have not been real for a long time' (p. 2).

My annoyance with Miller's statements stemmed from my discomfort at realising I *had* been affected by my parents' behaviour, despite my resolute belief that I had left my past and its negative impact behind me. Reading Miller's book was a true light-bulb experience; it was as if cataracts had fallen from my eyes. A writer's words really resonate when a shiver of recognition runs through the reader as they read. Such was my experience reading Miller.

In my mind I ran through the various flash points with my children: arguments about pocket money; fiery, loud anger if Kev used bad language; contemptuous tones when scolding; too much scolding; too high expectations, etc. Since reading Miller's work, I have been listening to myself as I talk to my children and applying 'verbal brakes' when my utterances are just echoes of parental influences rather than anything that will help or guide my children. Miller showed me that the relationship between me and my children is being influenced and driven by the relationship that existed between me and my own parents. The way in which a parent has been parented will determine their inherited style of parenting.

2. *Homecoming* by John Bradshaw
In his 1992 bestseller, *Homecoming: Reclaiming and Healing your Inner Child*, counsellor, theologian and television host John Bradshaw writes about the impact of parental abuse and neglect on personality development. He writes of the lifelong effects of being reared in an alcoholic household, a situation in which he offered deeply personal insights. His own father had been addicted to alcohol and eventually abandoned the

family. The section I gained most from was 'Toxic Shame'. Shame is something I have long grappled with as a result of my own experience of parental alcoholism. Bradshaw writes that: 'With guilt, you've done something wrong: but you can repair that – you can do something about it. With toxic shame, there's something wrong with *you* and there's nothing you can do about it, you *are* inadequate and defective. Toxic shame is the core of the wounded child' (p. 47).

Bradshaw offers exercises to help repair what he calls our 'inner child'. Firstly, he asks us to complete questionnaires in relation to our stages of development, such as how we felt about ourselves as pre-school children. The exercises are soul-searching, and to be done with caution. Reclaiming your inner child involves going back through your developmental stages and finishing any unfinished business. Bradshaw suggests forming a vision of what it was like for you when you were at each of the four developmental stages: (1) 9 months to 18 months; (2) 3 years to 6 years; (3) 6 years to puberty; and (4) 13 years to 26 years.

Questions are posed, the answers to which indicate the extent to which your inner child was wounded. Bradshaw includes 'corrective' exercises that include self-care, such as hanging in a hammock for a long time or letting someone give you a manicure or do your hair. He also writes of 'establishing your own separate domain' and outlines a set of rules, such as 'Some of my time is my own. I may or may not share it with you.' *Homecoming* is a tough book to read but worth the effort in helping us to identify how our parents influenced us.

3.   *Choice Theory: A New Psychology of Personal Freedom* by William Glasser
'What helped me most was the work of William Glasser – *Choice Theory*. I struggled to deal with my daughter's issues. What I really needed to do was deal with myself.' An AP speaking about her relationship with her adult adopted daughter.

William Glasser, psychiatrist and lecturer, developed the concept of Choice Theory, which holds that we make choices because our motivations are from within us and not from outside us. In his book, Glasser writes: 'Choice Theory explains that, for all practical purposes, we choose everything we do, including the misery we feel. Other people can neither make us miserable nor make us happy. All we can get from them is information. Choice Theory shows us we are much more in control of our lives than we realize' (1998, p. 4).

Glasser believes that most of what we do is as a result of the choices we make (except in extreme cases such as a gun to the head or an attack with overwhelming force). He gives the example of a ringing phone, which we automatically feel we should answer. But Glasser points out we *choose* to answer it, we are conditioned to believe we *must* answer. If we choose not to answer it and continue what we are doing, a disruption does not occur. We can ring back at a later time, or we can pick the phone up immediately and answer. This example can be applied to almost any aspect of our lives – our reaction to a son refusing to do his homework, a daughter not helping around the house, a car tailgating us on the motorway – we can choose how to react and that choice impacts on our wellbeing. The concept of choice is empowering and one that has helped me understand how many aspects of my life are due to my own choices. For example, choosing not to become angry and judgemental during interactions with my children has opened a whole new way of parenting. Glasser's theory encourages us to look at life from a whole new perspective.

Step Two – Parenting Style
The reading of any of the above books will be a trigger for step two of self-evaluation. As our own parenting style is influenced by our experience of being parented, pondering the following questions will open up some thoughts on parenting style. As highlighted by Alice Miller and John Bradshaw, the attitudes foisted on APs by their own parents will influence how they parent their own child.

Did my parents show affection to me?
Were my parents happy in their marriage?
How was I disciplined as a child; was there physical punishment?
Am I close to my parents (if still living) now?
Am I nursing unresolved issues from my childhood, such as the effect of parental alcohol dependency?
Would I describe my childhood as a happy one?
How do my own parents feel about adoption?

The influence of the APs' parents is also referred to in H. David Kirk's *Shared Fate* as follows: 'The couple contemplating adoption is thus probably sensitive to the way their parents overtly or covertly regard adoption' (p. 18).

Our parents' attitude to adoption will influence *our* attitude because we, in turn, inherit our parents' values. If your parents disagree with adoption and advocate for silence and secrecy on your child's adoption status, then this will impact on your own openness with your child.

Step Three – The Loss of Blood Links and When to Talk about Adoption

Pondering the impact of the loss of blood links is a vital part of self-evaluation. Both AP and child have lost blood links. Reflection by APs on their own loss will help them understand their child's loss.

For example, when I reflect on the absence of physical similarities between me and my children and what that means to me, how the sharing of family likeness does not exist and what sadness, if any, that brings up for me, a start has been made toward understanding, in turn, the loss my child feels. I have grown up with bits of me everywhere: relatives with similar facial features, voice, hair colour, height and personality characteristics. It is easy for anyone with a nearby biological family to take for granted the presence of people with similar looks and characteristics. It is then also true that they might have no understanding of how it feels to not have people around who look the same as you. Reflecting on my own loss of blood connection by not giving birth helps me empathise with how my child might feel. Betty Lifton, adoption author and counsellor, writes in a 2010 article published in the online journal *Psychoanalytic Inquiry*, of the 'ghosts' in the adoptive relationship:

> The APs are accompanied by the ghost of the perfect baby they were not able to conceive, who was stillborn or who died young. That child would have looked like them, shared their talents, and fulfilled their aspirations. They may try to ignore the ghost of the birth mother of the child they are raising, but she has a way of materializing, especially when the child screams: 'You are not my real mother!' One adoptive mother called her 'the ghost in the closet.'

Reflecting on and mulling over the loss of blood connection helps us to recognise the child's emotions and empathise with them. This helps us understand why they might act out as a consequence of their loss of blood connection.

Much has been written about the correct age to start talking to the child about their adoption. Often, APs feel their pre-teen child isn't ready to talk about adoption because they are too young. The difficulty arises when years of not raising the subject of adoption have slipped past and the child becomes a teenager, where all the pressures of adolescence come into play. Adopted people write about childhoods spent wanting passionately to talk to APs about their origins but finding the subject was not a welcome one. APs may feel their child isn't ready to talk about adoption, but the reality is that it is often *the AP who isn't ready*. Self-evaluation will prepare the AP to deal with the challenge of rearing their child.

Some questions for APs to ponder:

How do I feel about the complexity of adoption?
How do I feel about the lack of blood links?
How do I react to my child when they ask: 'Where is my real mother?'
What if my child screams: 'You're not my real mother'?
How does the expression 'real mother' make me feel?
What does the concept of talking to my child from early infancy about adoption feel like for me?
How would I feel if my child shared with others the details of their birth family?
How does it feel to know that my child needs, like oxygen, to have some sort of connection, however tenuous, with their birth family?

Adoption is a life-long journey. As the child grows, the need to be able to talk about adoption grows too. This need can only be satisfied by parental understanding and efforts to have the adoption conversation. Through self-examination, we can exorcise ghosts in the closet. Irrespective of the challenges presented by adoptive parenting, having undertaken the three steps as outlined above, I can write with conviction that the AP who looks closely at themselves and openly admits how they feel about adoption will be able to overcome the difficulties and help their child achieve self-actualisation and healing.

Acceptance of Infertility

The AP is unable to pass on their genes. As APs, we must examine how much the disappointment of infertility impacts on our relationship with our child. The AP nurses the grief of infertility, a grief that is compounded by the obvious differences in personality and appearance between the AP and child. Self-evaluation and reflection will help us deal with issues such as the acceptance of infertility.

Adoptive Parents Reaching Out for Help – Post Adoption Support

Eventually you are blessed and lucky enough to fulfil your dream of becoming a parent. The last thing that you then want to admit, having portrayed yourself to the health authorities as a model prospective parent and a paragon of parental love and superhuman ability, is that you now need help with your adoptive parenting, especially as this is the same health authority that you received a declaration of suitability from.

Patricia Irwin Johnson writes:

> Having been given the seal of approval as perfect parents, they [APs] were afraid to go to their adoption workers to ask questions about what they were experiencing, because they feared that in doing so they could risk losing their child by admitting to their caseworker – the most powerful person they had had contact with in their lives – that there were problems (1992, p. 218).

For prospective APs, the sole focus is on obtaining the declaration of suitability. There is very much a 'before' and 'after' aspect – an AP cannot know what to expect until their adopted child is living with them and the uniqueness of their needs and personality traits become evident.

The post-adoption societal aura of 'You are the lucky one, you have the child, get on with it' seems to me to be one of the main reasons why many APs struggle on in silence. Admitting that their child is a challenge to rear at times can be tough for APs who had to present themselves in the best possible light during assessment; it can often feel like an admission of failure. The negotiation of role handicap as experienced by APs post adoption is an area largely ignored by the health authority. This shortage of support is not solely pertinent to Ireland. John Houghton, British AP and author of an unflinchingly honest memoir of adopting three children from the care system, writes of his efforts to obtain post-adoption support: 'We tried to find help by ringing Social Services to ask about post-adoption service. The response was discouraging: "Post? Oh, you mean 'after'. No, there's nothing like that"' (2006, p. 162). Houghton describes eventually finding help from a sympathetic social worker who worked part-time and was 'half of the entire Post Adoption support unit'.

Search and reunion services also fall within the gamut of post-adoption support. Search services for adoptees born outside of Ireland are non-existent in Ireland. While a contact register (the National Adoption Contact Preference Register or NACPR) has been in existence in Ireland since 2005, this register only supports people born in Ireland. In consideration of the 5,000 people who have been adopted from abroad between 1991 and 2015 (Adoption Authority of Ireland), the provision of regulated search services is necessary.

Efforts to establish accessible and appropriately skilled post-adoption services around Ireland are ongoing. Currently, Barnardos (serving Dublin, Kildare and Wicklow) provides the only official service in the country, which is staffed with trained adoption professionals. Support groups have set up an umbrella organisation to highlight the need for the provision of post-adoption services throughout the rest of the country. See the Adoption Authority of Ireland Network of Adoption Support Groups (NASGI).

My Experience of Personal Therapy

'In order to become whole we must try, in a long process, to discover our own personal truth, a truth that may cause pain before giving us a new sphere of freedom.' Alice Miller, *The Drama of Being a Child* (1987, p. 2).

I am a latecomer to the wonders of personal therapy. Until I sought bereavement counselling after my sister died in 2006, the concept of sharing my innermost thoughts or exploring the circumstances and events of my childhood with a stranger was not a practice I had ever considered. My past, in particular, was not a topic I wished to delve into. Up until then, I very much aspired to the saying that 'the past is a foreign country, they do things differently there'. What was done was done and I had moved on.

Burying the events of the past and moving on regardless was one of the overriding themes of the US smash-hit series, *Mad Men*. In the scene where Don Draper (Jon Hamm) visits Peggy Olsen (Elizabeth Moss) in hospital after she has given birth to a child as a result of an affair with a married man, a situation particularly frowned upon in the sixties (the decade in which the show is set), he shares some of his worldly wisdom: 'Move forward. This never happened. It will shock you how much it never happened.'

I can identify with Draper's tenet. I resolutely refused to let my past bother me in any way, and in many ways, it has not mattered at all. If I did not think about my father's alcoholism, my sibling with a disability and the early death of my mother and father, it would let go of me and I would then keep it under control and under wraps. If I needed to talk about any aspect of my past, which sometimes I did in a cursory and often mocking way, my sister was a willing listener and participant.

Small wonder then that when Theresa died I was bereft beyond words. Without realising it, I had become totally dependent on my sister to bolster my feelings about the past, reliant on her understanding to help me mull over past events, needing her to confirm a memory for me or keep me in touch with the finer details of my heritage. Without realising it, I *had* been processing my past, but only within the confines of our bond as sisters who had shared experiences.

After her death, my inner world came crashing down. Seeking out bereavement counselling led me to discuss family events with an objective stranger and led me to open a Pandora's box of suppressed emotions. Talking about the past to Theresa had ensured that there was no real openness – I was keeping my truth within the circle of the family. Talking about the past to my therapist, someone separate from the world where it all happened, allowed me to freely express my thoughts to an objective, detached listener.

Ongoing, substantial therapy was not something I had set out to engage in. If someone had told me a few years ago I would spend 50 hours in front of a therapist I would have told them they were mad. Me, 50 hours of therapy? No way! However, I wanted to qualify as a psychotherapist, so I had no option but to attend. Substantial engagement in personal therapy is a pre-requisite for training to be a therapist. At first, it seemed like a racket. Students being compelled to attend therapy? Surely it was just a way of generating business for other (accredited) therapists? Yet, the outcome of this 'forced' therapy is the justification and the rebuttal of my grumbles about racketeering.

After hours in the company of my sympathetic and empathic counsellor, I can confidently say that engaging in ongoing, regular therapy has changed my life. Regular attendance allows for slow and meticulous dissection of thoughts, concepts and attitudes, as well as an exploration of how the conditioning of childhood influences one's perception of and reaction to life events. We all know that shit happens; it's how we deal with it that counts.

Personal therapy forced me to stare into my past and acknowledge that what happened back there made me the person I am today. Therapy led me to realise that parental depression and alcoholism had a profound effect on how I was formed. Talking about it made it all the more acceptable and forgivable. My own acceptance of me, as I am, is the live proof of the relevance of this exercise. I now look at people with empathy and try to walk in their shoes. Things that previously made me angry, I have now become more philosophical about. Now that I understand the influence parental anger had on me and my development, I look at previous irritants in a new light.

The most significant change has been in my approach toward my children. Hughes and Baylin write of the impact of the parental brain on the parent/child relationship: 'Attachment-focused therapists and trauma specialists strongly recommend that parents find ways to come to terms with their own past experiences and to defuse the negative potential for unresolved painful memories to disrupt their parenting and their kids' development' (2012, p. 41). I noted the tone of my own voice, an irritated, loud timbre that seemed reserved for Kev and Tatiana when I was in 'nag' mode; instead of firm, rational, parentally responsible instructions and responses, there were loud, angry exhortations.

I explored anger in the therapy room, reflecting on my father's intimidating disposition within our family unit, and I had a light-bulb moment: I was reliving his anger when I was speaking to my children. The anger he projected on to me was being projected on to Kev and Tatiana. This was an extraordinary discovery, especially as I explored the concept of control and how important control is for someone who has been raised in a chaotic, alcohol-dominated environment as I was.

Janet G. Woltitz describes the impact of being reared in an alcoholic home. She talks of the 'fear that if you are not in charge, if a change is made, abruptly, quickly, without warning, you will lose control of your life' (1983, p. 73). She also writes that 'Misery is familiar and you have learned how to deal with distress. Life going really well is unfamiliar to you, so you don't know how to manage it' (p. 115).

Hughes and Baylin write that 'parents who were exposed to high levels of adversity in early childhood or have experienced high levels of trauma earlier in life are likely to exhibit this kind of inflexible parenting due to compromised functioning of the executive brain system' (p. 78). Once I accepted that the experiences of my childhood were influencing how I was parenting my children, I was able to question myself when on the cusp of a heated dispute with them. This questioning of whether the matter was worth a row or if it was in fact just me reliving the anger spilt on me as a child was the basis for the strengthening of our relationship.

My ability to calm myself and remind myself that I am transferring anger I experienced in my early life on to them has been the greatest gift I could have given myself and my family. Ability to compromise and remain calm are the gifts I have received. I thank the self-evaluation in the confidential sanctuary of therapy for that.

Inside the Counselling Room

My first ever counselling session was with Bereavement Ireland after my sister died. In a little room in my local parish office, I was able to grieve openly, soaking tissue after tissue as I mourned the loss of my beloved sister. Trying to grieve at home was nigh impossible as I was conscious of the impact of my grief on Kev and Tatiana (then aged five and eight), who were already hurting from an earlier loss (separation at birth) as well as grieving for their beloved aunt. The result was a bottling up of my grief, which sat like a ball of hardened cement on my chest, ready to explode at the smallest reminder that my sister had died. Patricia, my counsellor, listened quietly and attentively to my grief as well as giving me tips on how to face the tasks that arise upon losing a loved one. Writing replies to sympathy letters I had received, how to help my brother-in-law distribute memorial cards and how to prepare myself for uttering the words 'my sister died' were just a few of those tasks.

One of my biggest torments in the year after Theresa's death was bumping into casual acquaintances while in the supermarket or at activities with the children. When an acquaintance would attempt to sympathise with me, I would dissolve into tears. I would then have to witness their embarrassment at my very public display of grief, something that added further to my distress. Discussing these events with Patricia helped me deal with my grief. From those eight sessions, I learned the inestimable value of talking through issues with an objective and sympathetic stranger. The relief and comfort gained was immense, much more impactful and useful than I anticipated. I, who had been up to then judgemental of people who went to counsellors, as if in some way they were weaker than me. I didn't tell anyone I was attending bereavement counselling, fearing that others would judge me as I have previously judged others.

In the year after my sister died, I faced a further life-altering dilemma. I had been on a career break from my job in banking for nearly three years. I was now facing the prospect of having to decide whether to return to work. In the wake of Theresa's death, I engaged in much soul searching. What was life all about anyway, when someone could be here one moment and gone the next? Was I emotionally able to return to my job in the bank, to attend and deal with customer demands all day? Could I face having to hand over the wonderful freedom of the life I had created as a homemaker to return to being chained to a perennially loaded-down-with-tasks bank desk? My reflecting on my life was not surprising given the shock of Theresa's sudden death. However, the prospect of actually leaving my job forever, never returning, walking away from my life-long role (well, since age seventeen anyway) as a banker brought me out in a cold sweat.

The Wonder of Self-Evaluation

I hadn't bargained for the abject devastation I felt when I told myself: 'I'm leaving my bank job forever.' It was easy being on a career break with the reassuring shadow of a job in the background. Saying 'I'm returning to my job in a few years' was infinitely easier than 'I'm finished working in the bank.' Resigning from my job meant I was no long a bank official, no longer the person I used to be. At that point, it seemed that the important parts of my life were breaking off and leaving me: I had lost my beloved sister to cancer and now my career was slipping away. A chance meeting with a former bank official (to whom I am eternally grateful) sent me down the road of contacting the bank's Employee Assistance service and eventually a meeting with a counselling psychologist called Catherine.

When I sat down with Catherine in her consulting room in Dublin, I assumed she would be working with me to establish a way in which I could reignite my enthusiasm for the banking life. I expected a conversation similar to previous conversations with Human Resources, reviewing my 'skill set' and trying to match it against the 'requirements' of the bank. Nothing could be further from what actually happened. After taking the usual swathe of personal details, Catherine opened the session with a question: 'What was it like for you during your childhood? What were your father and mother like?' I can still remember those words and the panic that poured over me like a bucket of icy water.

'Pardon?' I stuttered.

This was the FIRST time EVER anyone, in such a non-judgemental, private and caring setting where I didn't have to be hypervigilant and cautious about my response, had so directly and specifically asked me about my childhood.

Theresa was the only person with whom I had talked about Drumrookel, Co. Leitrim, where we were reared – she who was there and had endured it all with me but was now gone forever. Talking to a stranger about such buried stuff? Catherine repeated her question. A sob constricted my speech. 'Please don't ask me about that,' I begged. 'Anything but that.'

Her kind, sympathetic face curled enquiringly: 'But why?'

For several minutes, I sobbed, unable to speak, as the demons of my childhood emerged and flew around our heads. Eventually I found my voice and the events in Drumrookel during my childhood surfaced in

Catherine's therapy room like black shapeshifters, swishing and darting. I cried, bundles of soaking tissues piled beside me as I talked about my father's alcoholism and the impact of his irrational temper and mood swings on the family.

I talked about things that I had never enunciated to anyone before, besides Theresa, my loss of whom was colouring and still is colouring every aspect of my life. When she died, a chunk of my past died too. Talking to Catherine released the genie from the bottle. The unexpected examination of my childhood awakened me to the comfort of self-expression in the presence of an objective, impartial listener.

I had been referred to Employee Assistance to tease out why I was so devastated about resigning from my job and had unexpectedly stepped into the landmine of my past. As a result of the counselling sessions, I could see that getting the job in the bank, all those years ago at seventeen, had led me to a new 'family'. The bank represented a separate family for me. Working had given me a fresh lease of life and sanctuary from the chaos of my father's alcohol-fuelled behaviour. The welcoming nature of the staff, the sharing of a flat with two girls who worked in the branch with me, the acceptance of me and the complete lack of knowledge of my family situation allowed me to establish a separate identity. I was mingling with people in whose company I felt no shame, who did not know that my father was 'fond of the drink'. I was Mari, the Sligo-based bank official, who was a committed worker. Small wonder then that having to make a decision about walking away from what had been my second family for two and a half decades wrought such distress upon me.

Counselling helped me to figure that out and see through my reluctance to leave the bank, even though I knew I was ready to leave, having done as much with my bank career as I was able. In the counselling room, I had named what was wrong and in doing so was able to deal with it. The catharsis brought incomparable solace and a belief in the power of self-expression without judgment. By the time I had my fourth session, I had sent my letter of resignation to the regional manager, albeit still with sadness in my heart. The sessions with Catherine not only cleared up my complicated emotions around my job resignation but also illuminated for me the value of a therapeutic relationship. The saying 'It's good to talk' became a personal mantra for me and eventually led me into counselling and psychotherapy as a career.

The Wonder of Self-Evaluation

The Adventure of Being a Child

'They fuck you up, your mum and dad, they may not mean to, but they do. They fill you with the faults they had. And add some extra, just for you.' Philip Larkin, 'This Be the Verse'.

Philip Larkin's 'This Be the Verse' was a featured poem in the late Anthony Cronin's poetry column in the *Sunday Independent* in August 2014. Cronin's introduction to the poem was insightful in its acknowledgment of the validity of the expressions within Larkin's writing:

> Larkin was a truth-teller. He uncovered emotions and states of mind which often lie beneath those we feel or think we feel or pretend to feel. He had no truck with the visionary, the inspired or the numinous, which he distrusted. His best poems are examples of the fact that, as Emerson said, the truth once stated is instantly received.

Cronin's understanding of Larkin's sentiments is refreshing – commentary on the influence of parenting on our personalities and mental well-being is rare enough; yet here is pointing out how he 'instantly received' Larkin's poem because it was 'the truth once stated'. The extent to which behaviour is influenced by parenting is so all-encompassing that it's notable how comparatively little acknowledgement there is of it. As grimly espoused by Larkin, issues are passed from generation to generation, and yet, as enunciated by John Bowlby (cited in J. Holmes, 1993): 'Man and woman power devoted to the production of material goods counts a plus in all our economic indices. Man and woman power devoted to the production of happy, healthy and self-reliant children in their own homes does not count at all' (p. 201). It is difficult to read 'This Be the Verse' and not react: either in annoyance and denial or with a belt of sadness at the memories it evokes. The line: 'Man hands on misery to man, it deepens like a coastal shelf' offers very little in the way of hope or redemption and portrays parental love and acceptance, something that we presume is automatically present in parent-child relationships, as constituting something that is far from guaranteed.

Examining my past and how I was parented stoked long-buried memories and accompanying emotions that rose like ghouls. Alice Miller writes of people who enter therapy with a belief (which they grew up with) that their childhood was happy and protected and that the repression of their real history has been so complete that their illusion of a good childhood can be maintained with ease. While I can describe my childhood as largely happy and protected, there were aspects of it that I needed to look at and understand. Counselling helped me to do this.

My Childhood

'Experience has taught us that we have only one enduring weapon in our struggle against mental illness: the emotional discovery of the truth about the unique history of our childhood.' Alice Miller (p. 1).

Shortly after they got married in the fifties, my father and mother, like many Irish of their era, immigrated to England. Three of their children were born in England: my older brother, younger sister and myself. The fourth child, my younger brother, was born in Ireland. My mother, my two siblings and I returned to Leitrim in 1964, when I was three years old. My father remained on in England for five years while my mother set up home on our newly purchased farm in Drumrookel near Carrick-on-Shannon. As a child I missed my father and remember standing against the front door, blocking his exit, as he left after a visit to go back to work in England. For me, my father worked in England simply to provide for us financially. Later, in the light of his patent unhappiness and the tension and disagreements between my parents, I realised his absence from the family home was very likely an escape for him from the demands and strictures of family life. It was also likely that my mother was more content by herself for those few years, away from my father's drunken antics and mood swings. My father returned to Ireland in 1969, and their constant, loud arguments disrupted the previous peacefulness of our home; those arguments remain an indelible memory.

I grew up aware of discord between my parents and rarely witnessed them laughing together or visibly enjoying each other's company. They never called each other by their first names, and my mother would refer to my father as 'him' when she spoke of him to us. In *The Spinning Heart* by Irish novelist Donal Ryan, the character Bobby Mahon describes his father in a way that mirrored my experience. As I read Ryan's description, recognition coursed through me. I wasn't the only one with a 'walking on eggshells' childhood, even if this description was just from a character in a novel:

> I'll never forgive him for the killing sting of his tongue. He ruined every day of our lives with it. Drunk, he was leering and silent and mostly asleep. Sober, he was a watcher, a horror of a man who missed nothing and commented on everything. Nothing was ever done right or cooked right or said right or bought right or handed to him properly or ironed straight or finished off fully with him. We couldn't breathe right in a room with him. We couldn't talk freely or easily (2012, p. 18).

Much of my childhood interaction with my mother was dominated by her need to vent about my father's behaviour and realistically, who else could she vent to? In Ireland in the sixties and seventies, if the husband owned a farm and earned a wage, the attitude toward the wife was 'put up and shut up'. To be fair to my father, his work ethic and responsibility toward providing for his family was a positive aspect of his personality and deserving of acknowledgement. Irrespective of the behaviour exhibited by her spouse in the privacy of the family home, my mother and the wives of her time were expected to be grateful that they had husbands who were able to support them and their children. However, this meant that I was the ear for my mother's understandable frustration and anxiety toward my father's alcohol-related behaviour. From as young as eight years of age, I listened to my mother's long-winded tirades about my father's doings.

Both Miller and Bradshaw, cited in the previous section, write about the child becoming an adult early in life. Being expected to display a grown-up demeanour dominated my childhood. I had to take on the role of listener for my mother, who of course couldn't confide in anyone else about the distress and misery of her marriage. She also had a son (my older brother) with a disability and was aware that she would have limited options if she had taken the monumental (and in those times largely unheard of) step of leaving the marriage. My brother needed ongoing help and support and my mother was preoccupied with ensuring he was cared for, on top of all her other responsibilities as a wife, mother and farmer. My father earned a wage and my mother was financially dependent on him. Once, she spoke about walking away from the marriage. I was about nine years old at the time. I remember advising her in a staunch tone to leave my father while terror was churning inside me. I prayed that she wouldn't as I couldn't even imagine what that might bring in terms of upheaval, devastation and shame. Anxiety and fear pervaded a large part of my childhood.

As I lay in bed at night, fearfully awake and awaiting my father's return from the pub, when raised voices would invariably start up, I would cower under the covers in anticipation of what I might hear. Daily I distracted myself by reading book after book and avidly watching romantic movies with classic happy-ever-after endings. Much of my childhood was spent in hypervigilance awaiting the outbreak of the next alcohol-driven barrage from my father.

Dr Garett O'Connor cites John Waters, Irish journalist and social commentator, in a 2012 article published in *Irish America* magazine: 'Drinking in Ireland is not simply a convivial pastime, it is a ritualistic alternative to real life, a spiritual placebo, a fumble for eternity, a longing for heaven, a thirst for return to the embrace of the Almighty [...] and evidence of a deep hole in the Irish psyche which only alcohol can fill.' On reflection, it seems to me that my father was eternally trying to dull some pain, some emotional hollowness that he did not feel encouraged enough to reveal. He occasionally spoke of being beaten as a child, citing an older relative who would, at random and without warning, whack the side of his head with a heavy walking stick. He also alluded, in obtuse terms, to being subjected to inappropriate fondling by a priest when he was a child; this was something I didn't ever get to the point of asking more about. If my parents had lived longer, long enough to witness the tumultuous changes and expositions of abuse within the Catholic Church and the consequent changing of attitudes, it is possible that both of them could have had stories to tell. But this is all just supposition and their secrets are gone to the grave with them.

Heavy drinking has been a feature of Irish culture for decades, and this has not changed. O'Connor writes of an Irish legacy of shame, which is a

… net effect of religious persecution, land rape, extreme poverty and intermittent abuse of military power by English colonists in

Ireland during 700 years of continuous occupation, producing a national inferiority complex in Irish Catholics which I identify as cultural malignant shame, characterised by chronic fear, suppressed rage, self-loathing, procrastination, low self-esteem, false pride and a vulnerability to use alcohol as remission for suffering (2012).

I recognise all of this in my father and by extension, in myself. My father's alcoholism did not make him stand out in the community. While his drink-related behaviour filled me with shame, he was never spoken of amongst the extended family as an alcoholic. Hard drinkers were everywhere, and most families at that time had at least one if not more loved ones who were abusing alcohol, a fact that fuelled a tacit acceptance of alcoholism as an immoveable feature of our culture.

During a play therapy workshop, undertaken as part of my psycho-therapy training, I played an art therapy game with miniature toy animals as part of a therapeutic exercise that unexpectedly unearthed some subconscious thoughts. Play and art therapy allows the participant to express feelings through play and drawing, and in the case of an adult, will help to illustrate childhood thoughts and fears. Without dwelling on what I was actually trying to do, I found myself creating a set-piece with the miniatures. I arranged smaller animals, such as dogs, sheep, cats and squirrels in a huddle and had them circled by two tigers and three lions while other large but not as threatening animals (elephants and giraffes) stood by and observed. A fellow student, Ann, was in my group, and interpreted my toy-animal display as a clear message from my child-hood. 'It's obvious, Mari, that you felt something was going on and others stood by and did nothing.' While at no time in my childhood do I remember feeling that others should have helped me, it is possible that subconsciously I did feel my father's alcohol-related behaviours and my mother's defencelessness against him happened in plain sight of our extended family and neighbours. I hold no bitterness for any perceived lack of action. What could realistically have been done? Intervening in a family where dysfunction is present is a complex process, even now. Back then it was unheard of. Families just struggled on and extended family members rarely interfered, unless it was obvious that someone's life was in clear danger. Yet, to my amazement, a casual exercise in art therapy allowed me to express a subconscious belief that a childhood need was being ignored.

My Parents' Work Ethic

Both my parents had strong work ethics. My mother was eternally active with the farm and housework. Irish poet Mary O'Donnell pays tribute to the undocumented work of women in her 1998 poem 'Unlegendary Heroes', and brings to mind my mother and her capacity for work:

> Kathleen McKenna, Annagola,
> who was able to wash a week's sheets, shirts
> and swaddling, bake bread and clean the house
> all of a Monday.

> Phyllis McCrudden, Knockaphubble,
> who buried two husbands, reared five children,
> and farmed her own land.

I have a memory of my mother's slight frame buckling under a mound of hay strapped to her back as she moved, head pushed forward on frost-bound mornings, through the gate in front of our house on her way to feed the cattle. My mother milked and fed the cows daily; walked the length and breadth of our fifty-acre farm; saved the hay in summer; cycled fourteen kilometres round trip to the nearest town, returning with laden bags; washed clothes for six people by hand; and cooked all the meals. All the while she was rearing a son with a disability as well as three other children, and in addition to this, was coping with the stress of an alcoholic husband. I suppose keeping busy was my mother's way of getting through. In spite of all this, my mother's sense of optimism was palpable. The demands of her life did not prevent her from being an attentive, responsive, loving mother. The difficulties presented by life didn't hinder her raucous sense of humour either; her wheezy laughter at some snippet of neighbourhood gossip or a television comedy sketch (Benny Hill was a particular favourite) often rang around the kitchen.

My father was a diligent, industrious worker, holding down a full-time job in Leitrim County Council until he died, as well as keeping busy on the farm, repairing machinery, ploughing the fields to plant vegetables and engaging in renovations and repairs to the house. He was a functioning alcoholic: able to carry on his daily duties while engaging in substance abuse. Despite the difficulties wrought on me by my father's actions, I respected and loved him. My relationship with him was a mixture of admiration for his fatherly skills (he held down a job, he could taxi me to nights out, repair the television, do multiple home improvements and tell funny stories) and contempt for his drunken aggression toward my mother and the rest of us whenever the mood took him. This conflicted regard stayed with me for as long as he lived. During occasions of great togetherness, so rare they stuck in my mind, I do recall us having intimate father/daughter chats. I remember when I would return from work in Sligo for the weekend to find him sitting under the reading light in the corner of our living-room, glasses on, reading the newspaper or *Readers Digest*. My mother would accost me as soon as I stepped into the scullery and delegate me the task of joining my father in the sitting room: 'Sit down and talk to him, that will put him in good humour.' I would duly lower myself into the chair next to him and ask how it was going. He would lift his eyes from his book, peer over his glasses at me, and say something like 'The wanderer returns' or 'The big bank woman from Sligo is here.' We would chat about books or telly or something that was in the news or I would share some light-hearted work-related snippet with him. My father's need to connect was the same as any other human. Bursts of decency, which frequently flashed through the belligerence, told of an intelligent, insightful, witty man who was (very likely) damaged by (alluded to only) events of his childhood. The current emphasis on mental health issues may have provided an epiphany for my father and, had he lived to see it, an opportunity to explore his childhood and what happened to him.

My Mother's Death

In 1987 my mother was diagnosed with malignant melanoma, a form of skin cancer. A large freckle had become infected (cancerous) and she had to have it removed from her arm. It's hard to describe the devastation of the arrival of terminal illness on the doorstep of a family already besieged by such emotional pressure. My mother did not tell my father that the GP had told her the freckle was cancerous. She was in the hospital for only a few days and had taken a lift from her sister-in-law to and from the hospital. She had not discussed any aspect of the procedure with her. Despite my awareness of my mother's reluctance to confide in my father, I knew that her illness could not be kept a secret from him. A few weeks after she returned from hospital, I told my father that the GP had said the freckle was cancerous and that was why it had been removed from her arm.

He became agitated when I mentioned cancer and urged me to contact the surgeon and get a post-operation report. I made the appointment and excused myself from work, where I left behind a chaotic cash-strewn desk, to meet with my mother's surgeon, a kindly, clear-skinned man who didn't mince his words. Not having thought much about cancer or having (back then) much experience of it in the family, I had somehow assumed there would be a hopeful prognosis.

The surgeon opened the conversation by saying he had tried to talk to my mother, but when he asked her what family member was with her so that he could inform the family member and her together, my mother had phlegmatically (the surgeon's description of my mother's tone) answered: 'I am with a friend,' and left without engaging in any discussion. The surgeon then told me what he had not told my mother. His words have stayed with me. 'I fear the cancer has spread. Melanoma spreads like wildfire. I believe she will have a lump under her arm soon. I give her between eighteen months and two years to live.' I burst into sobs in front of this stranger before returning to the pandemonium of work; a large cash discrepancy necessitated everyone's transactions to be double-checked before leaving, while I stood impotently at my desk, silent with shock and unable to concentrate. I was immediately conflicted as a result of being the receiver of this horrific information. My mother's insistence on privacy made me aware that she would not want me to talk about the cancer, even with my father. However, such news could not be hidden for long.

In the aftermath of learning of my mother's prognosis, realisation of the fragility of life and its transience coursed like ice through my veins. Up until then I was the daughter, the child of my mother and father. Suddenly I was the adult, the person in charge of the family secret, the bearer of the most catastrophic news. If anyone was to ask me at which point precisely I reached adulthood in the real, emotional sense, it was that day, when I was 27 years old, the day a surgeon told me my darling, beloved mother was dying.

After my meeting with the surgeon, I travelled to Drumrookel for a few days. I remember my first sighting of my mother since the surgeon's revelation on the state of her health – a revelation that still had not been made to her. How surreal to be told that your mother was terminally ill before she was informed. She was sitting on my father's handmade fuel box in the kitchen, mug of tea in hand, face pale and thin but happy as ever to see me and still there, still alive, still vitally present. A recurring dream – even now, twenty-eight years on – is that first sighting of my mother after I had heard of the terminal nature of her illness, after I had passed into adulthood, as I stepped through the kitchen door of Drumrookel. I regularly dream that she is still alive, still there when I go home for the weekend, sitting on the fuel box drinking tea, smiling, waiting for me.

I wanted to respect my mother's desire for privacy. When I broached the subject of the outcome of her procedure with her, her instruction was not to tell my father anything because he would be gossiping about her 'to all and sundry in the pub'. Not only was I the carrier of devastating news, but I was caught between my parents' dissension toward each other. However, a terminal illness was not something that could be kept secret from those close to her and her subsequent stays in hospital were evidence enough of the seriousness of the situation.

The final moments of my mother's life are forever enshrined in my mind. My father sat at the top of the hospital bed, his arm around my mother's shoulders, his head bent over hers. A stark portrayal of marriage, its complexities and contradictions, the closeness, the disdain, the love mixed with contempt and the impact of the glue of shared experience and memories – after a lifetime of disparaging and disrespecting my mother, my father was by her side, his arm supporting her, his cheek on the top of her head, until her last breath left her.

My Father's Last Year

In the year after she died, my mother's role in the core of the family unit was starkly illuminated. My father's presence always overshadowed my mother's. He was the one who made the most noise, who pulled rank as head of the household while my mother beavered away in the background. While my father had always been the one who featured as the leading figure in the family, it was my mother's death that splintered the family unit. Without her in Drumrookel, there was no longer a home as we knew it. Our central refuge was gone: the comfort, hospitality and warmth she facilitated by lighting a fire or filling the fridge was no longer present. The pivotal role she played in keeping the family together was not something I had ever thought about until those empty, dreary, cold months in the wake of her leaving us in March 1990. The extent to which my father had leaned on her only became apparent after her death, when it was too late for him to show appreciation for her. The loss of her was greater for him, in many ways, than us, the children; his loneliness after her death was incalculable. It was a real case of 'you don't know what you have got until it's gone'.

He went on sick leave from his job and was unable to do much; he struggled with feeding himself and being on his own. A few weeks after my mother's first anniversary mass, my father suffered a massive, fatal heart attack. My younger brother found him lying in the vegetable plot in front of our house. He had died just one year after my mother.

In the years since their deaths, being without them has allowed me to reflect on my relationship with them and their influence on me. There was something hurting my father greatly, some childhood experience that impacted on him. The realisation of parental damage repeating itself in the next generation has illuminated for me the truth of Philip Larkin's famous words about parents 'f**king you up': 'But they were f**ked up in their turn by fools in old-style hats and coats, who half the time were soppy-stern and half at one another's throats.' It is frightening to suppose that my own children could indeed be affected by issues passed via *my* grandparents to my parents and from me to my children: all the way through the generations.

The death of my parents taught me about loss. The lonely, directionless state of mind I experienced in the years after their death left me well-versed in what it might be like to lose a close and irreplaceable connection. The search for my children's birth parents was a task of adoptive parenthood that was made easier through the insight gained from the loss of my own parents.

Conclusion

Self-evaluation yields benefits for any parent – whether biological or adoptive. Our own unresolved issues have a heavy impact on how we rear our children. Adoption is different. Parenting a child who has been relinquished by his birth parents is different to parenting a child who is our own flesh and blood. Once adoption loss is acknowledged in a sensitive and empathic way by the AP, the child's development and well-being will be infinitely helped. Parenting is one of the most important jobs in the world. After all, parents are tasked with forming the next generation – what could be more important?

It is up to us to break the cycle as enunciated in Philip Larkin's poem: the emotional struggles endured by our own parents will stay, and unless ironed out, be passed on to our children, who in turn will pass them on to theirs. Searching our souls is an essential task. Reflection on our past is a start.

Chapter Six

HAVING THE ADOPTION CONVERSATION –
FORMING A BOND

'The wishful thinking on the part of many professionals
that denying the child the truth of his heritage would help
solidify his bond with the adoptive parents has been proven
wrong. It is now time to consider a whole new way of
approaching the adopted child.'
Betty J. Lifton, *Lost and Found: The Adoption Experience*

'All adopted kids wonder why.'
Cheri Register, *Are Those Kids Yours? American Families
with Children Adopted from Other Countries*

In the past, a view was held that the child should not be told the truth
of their background but instead lied to about their adoption and passed
off as their APs' biological child. American psychiatrist Thomas Harris
advocated for the keeping of the truth from the adopted child:

I honestly believe that it would be better for the child to be told
'yes, you grew in Mommy's tummy' even with implications of
dishonesty, than to go into great detail about growing in some
other mommy's tummy. If the little person is made to feel he
truly belongs, he will have a strong enough adult a little later in
life to comprehend why his parents may have lied to him: out of
love for him, to avoid burdening him with confusing and troubling truth (1973, pp. 194–95).

Adopted persons who are now adults have taught us important things about hiding 'confusing and troubling truth'. Secret-keeping is damaging and divisive, deception creates family mistrust and shame, and hiding the truth destroys family intimacy and security. Keefer and Schooler write that 'Above all, open, honest, sensitive communication about adoption and the past builds the gateway to healthy individual adjustment and family life' (2000, p. xiii).

In this chapter, I will explore how having the adoption conversation is as much a part of the bonding process between AP and child as other aspects of forming attachment, such as physical affection and regular presence. I will start with a summary of John Bowlby's attachment theory.

John Bowlby's Attachment Theory

(Citations on Bowlby in this section are taken from Jeremy Holmes, *John Bowlby and Attachment Theory*.)

'Mother love is as important for mental health as vitamins and proteins for physical health.' John Bowlby (1969, p. 35).

London-born, to an upper-middle-class family, John Bowlby (1907–1990) has been described as 'one of the three or four most important psychiatrists of the twentieth century' for his work on attachment in early childhood. Bowlby's attachment theory is one of the major theoretical developments in psychoanalysis. Ostensibly, Bowlby's theory is basic common sense and an affirmation of the premise on which maternal love is founded: that every child needs the love of a single, familiar primary carer. However, Bowlby has combined the rigorous scientific empiricism of ethology (the study of human character, its formation and evolution) with the subjective insights of psychoanalysis. The resulting theory has had an enormous impact on the fields of child development, social work, psychology, psychotherapy and psychiatry.

Bowlby's interest in attachment in infancy stems from his own childhood experience in his upper-middle-class family, where he saw his mother for one hour every day when he was an infant and was 'packed off' to boarding school when he was seven years old. He describes sending a young child to boarding school as something 'you would not do to a dog'. Bowlby was reared by his nanny and compares his feelings in relation to the departure of his nanny when he was four as being similar to losing his mother, as his nanny had been his primary care-giver.

Bowlby writes about the processes of attachment and loss from a position of personal experience. He provides experiential evidence, linking secure attachment in infancy with the development of 'autobiographical competence'. Bowlby claims that the theory of attachment can help us to understand society and its problems and suggests that if you go back into the childhood of any convicted psychopathic criminal, the deprivation of maternal love will undoubtedly have occurred. The core of this theory is that a child needs a primary care-giver in their life and that their mother, as the female, is more equipped with maternal attributes. The role of the father is less outlined in Bowlby's writing; he is primarily shown as a shadowy figure in the background, an aspect of attachment that places it at odds with the feminist ethos of equality in parenting and perpetuates the view that fathers 'opt out' when it comes to pulling their weight. The modern father, generally, would not concur with this view. Bowlby states that a child needs to be lifted, hugged, fed, kissed, made to feel safe, looked at, spoken to and caressed by the same primary giver – their mother. Separation in infancy from that care-giver brings on a host of emotional difficulties such as anxiety, sleeplessness, anger and delayed development, both emotional and intellectual. Bowlby's theory suggests that the rituals of attachment are of similar importance to food – a child needs to be hugged and caressed as much as they need to be fed. Bowlby writes that the prolonged deprivation of maternal care for a young child may have grave and far-reaching effects on their character and so, on the whole of their future life.

Despite his work being six decades old, Bowlby's theory of essential maternal love is as relevant as ever. Bruce Perry, adjunct professor of psychiatry at Northwestern University School of Medicine in Chicago, writes in his book, *Born for Love,* what he terms 'child-development illiteracy' – a lack of knowledge among parents of the infant's primal need for physical love, eye contact and touch. Perry also emphasises that bonding needs intense repetition. British psychoanalytic psychotherapist Sue Gerhardt writes in her 2004 book, *Why Love Matters: How Affection Shapes a Baby's Brain*, of the impact of the loving touch on the development of the young child. She states that those who are touched and held a great deal in babyhood, and who received plenty of attention in early life, have been found to be able to cope better with stress.

Music to the Ears of the Adoptive Parent

Bowlby centralises the importance of an 'attachment figure' rather than emphasising the need for a genetic connection, which is music to the ears of any AP. Bowlby posits that a child will attach to a loving carer as a natural consequence of physical affection, touch, presence, proximity and constant loving familiarity. Adoption and the impact of the blood link is not emphasised by Bowlby. Also, his theory is rooted in his personal experience of having been reared by a nanny. Bowlby's own story of attachment to his nanny as his main care-giver illustrates that a child will accept love from and become attached to a loving human, notwithstanding the absence of a genetic connection.

Definition of Attachment

John Bowlby describes attachment as a 'lasting psychological connectedness between human beings' (1969, p. 194). Attachment has been defined by psychologist Mary D. Ainsworth in an article entitled 'Attachment, Exploration and Separation' in the journal *Society for Research in Child Development* as 'an affectional tie that one person forms between himself and another specific one – a tie that binds them together and endures over time' (1970). Attachment is not just a connection between two people; it is a bond that involves a need for regular contact with that person and a feeling of distress during separation from that person. Ainsworth suggested three styles of attachment:

- Secure: constitutes the majority of children.
- Insecure avoidant: children who are distant from their attachment figure, likely to have been rejected by the primary care-giver in times of need.
- Insecure ambivalent/resistant: children who reject the primary care-giver during interaction yet cling to the care-giver on other occasions, resulting from an inconsistent level of response to their needs from the primary care-giver.

Making Strong Emotional Bonds

Bowlby theorises that attachment has an evolutionary aspect in that it aids survival. He wrote that: 'The propensity to make strong emotional bonds to particular individuals is a basic component of human nature' (p. 35). In forming a bond, Bowlby suggested four distinguishing characteristics of attachment that are also relevant in adoption attachment:

- Proximity maintenance: the desire to be near people whom we love and are attached to.
- Safe haven: being able to return to the person/attachment figure for safety and comfort when fear or threat is present.
- Secure base: the presence of the attachment figure provides a base of security from which the child is comfortable to explore the surrounding environment.
- Separation distress: when the attachment figure is not present, anxiety occurs as the child misses them.

Forming a Bond

'In a successful meeting, the social workers believed, adopters and child reached out to one another.' Barbara Melosh, *Strangers and Kin: The American Way of Adoption* (2002, p. 47).

In the majority of cases, forming an attachment is instinctive, and if someone was to ask, 'How do you know how to attach to a baby?' most would say it just happened, there was no rule book, simply a case of doing what comes naturally. To want to lift, hug and kiss a baby is instinct for most; it does not require an instruction manual. As I describe meeting with Kev, my first child, I realise it did all come naturally. Afterwards, however, as he grew older, I realised that I needed to know more to understand the needs of an adopted child.

While the characteristics of attachment are espoused by John Bowlby, some aspects are unique to the adoptive relationship. These aspects relate to the formation of the relationship with the child, the early days when the AP is learning to love the child, inducting the child into the AP's constellation of being and providing for the child a 'safe haven' as mentioned in Bowlby's characteristic of healthy attachment.

An Unforgettable Instant – Our First Meeting

The essential physical closeness of touch and eye contact when AP and child are getting to know each other is a crucial component of attachment. Every AP has her own story of what worked for her during those precious early bonding days when her child first arrived. For APs, in the absence of the automatic bonding of giving birth (although biological mothers will often admit to not immediately bonding with their biological child), there are differences. The challenge for the AP is the embracing and welcoming of a child already grown, already formed, with a place already staked out in the world. Like any other AP, the journey to my first child was filled with unforgettable moments. No other event is as outstanding in my memory as the first time I held Kev.

When Kev first appeared before me, every emotion within my psyche queued for prominence – the want to hold him, hug him, kiss him and most of all protect him. I used a sling to carry Kev out of the children's home, a tip an AP had shared with me. His little body was glued to mine, pressed close as if I was trying to replicate the experience of him being in my womb, as if I was trying to imagine myself giving birth to him.

At home, he was slung around my neck; my chin was close to the top of his head and he often stared up at me, as well as fixing his amazed blue eyes on the world around him – Newbridge, the Liffey River, the majestic trees, the incessant traffic. It was not long until he became too heavy to carry and his weight was straining against my neck. The swimming pool also offered chances for physical closeness as I carried him along, trying to get him accustomed to the buoyancy of the water as he learned to swim. Bonding happens just by doing what comes naturally: hugging and kissing your child as much as possible, maintaining eye contact, making funny faces to gain the child's attention and playing games. I'm mostly describing a *human attribute* – a natural inclination to want to touch and be close to another human. There are other specific techniques to help us bond with a child who has been relinquished at birth and spent time in institutional care.

Secure Attachment in Adoption: The Techniques

1. *Funnelling*
2. *Making a Child Your Own*
3. *Creating a Sanctuary to Deal with Loss*
4. *Using the PACE (Playfulness, Acceptance, Curiosity, Empathy) Model for Discipline and Bonding*
5. *Limiting Screen Technology*

1. *Funnelling*

The cornerstone of early attachment is the child's recognition of the APs as the primary people in their life. The limiting of physical contact between the newly adopted child and people other than the APs is recommended during the 'honeymoon' period (the early weeks of the child's adoption). The child and APs are getting to know one another, and this building of familiarity takes time. Where there is a large extended family and new faces introduced at a rapid rate to a newly adopted child, it is recommended that family members stay out of the way of the child until they have bonded with their APs. The act of requesting extended family to 'look but don't touch' can cause friction, especially where grandparents, for instance, really want (naturally) to lift and hug the newest family member. However, APs must be firm – the child is in the bonding process and everyone must play their part. In the interests of attachment, grannies, granddads, aunts, uncles etc. must try to give the newly formed family space – no physical contact and as much privacy as possible in the initial weeks of the child's arrival. Simply put, the child needs to know who's who. If a variety of faces are in their eyeline, lifting and hugging them as they try to assess who is their nearest and dearest, this may result in attachment being weaker than it should be, simply because the child isn't precisely sure who is their primary care-giver. A child who is exposed to an array of faces in the early days of their attachment process may not firmly attach, and who could blame them? Stepping into their shoes, it is easy to see how the child might find it difficult to figure out who is the primary care-giver. Instead, several new people lift them, hug them, speak to them, play with them and feed them. For secure attachment, the faces of their parents must be stamped onto their consciousness; the child must recognise them, incontrovertibly, as their primary carers. Otherwise, their attachment to their APs may not be secure and they may look for affection from any person who appears friendly. The child's attachment has been diluted by interactions with several friendly, affectionate people in a short period of time. Consequently, the child may develop indiscriminate affection – a symptom of insecure attachment denoted by frequently hugging, kissing or holding hands with people who are not well known, such as casual acquaintances, teachers or even strangers. The exhibiting of indiscriminate affection is one of the symptoms of insecure attachment and if it is not addressed, it may lead to a lack of bonding with the AP. Indiscriminate displays of affection are less likely to happen if funnelling is instituted in the 'honeymoon' period. Strong, secure attachment is the bedrock of adoptive relationships.

Anthony Watt, adoptive parent, writes in *The Guardian* of his experience with funnelling:

> Our social worker is adamant that we spend the first few months of life as a family as closely knit as possible: 'funnelling' is the technical term, and in practice it means we can't introduce any of our family or friends to our new children until they have had a chance to build an attachment with us, and only we can feed them, change them, bathe them, comfort them when they hurt or fulfil any of their myriad other needs. So while other new parents might call in their own mums and dads to take over some of the cooking, cleaning and playing, our children's new grandma is dropping off boxes of nappies under cover of darkness until she has permission to meet them. What a hoot!!! A selfish desire to show off our family (and maybe have a nap) aside, I actually buy into funnelling and know that it's really important for the children to build an attachment with us and that is easier if we keep everything low-key and focused on just them and us for a while (2011).

1.1. *My Experience of Funnelling by Default*

Sadly, as a result of bereavement and emigration, we had few family members around us and so our faces dominated the early weeks of

Kev's world. While at times it was lonely for us during those first weeks as we brooded on how few people we could share our joy with, the loneliness was balanced by a special, fabulous and undoubted magic in observing Kev's gradual attachment, like the slow opening of a flower's petals. The relaxing of his facial expression from tense to smiling, the development of his chuckles as he embraced hearty laughter, the softening of his crying from its initial distressed timbre and the holding of eye contact were all unmistakeable and wonderfully reassuring to witness. These early signs were undoubtedly the consequence of having only his APs in his world in those early weeks.

2. *Making a Child Your Own*

There is a dichotomy surrounding openness in adoption as APs learn to negotiate the balance between consistently acknowledging difference but not overemphasising adoption as the central part of the relationship. On one hand, openness is the lifeblood of the relationship between parent and child, and this depends on the willingness on behalf of the AP to have the adoption conversation. This openness is, however, an intensely private openness between parent and child. The adoption conversation is, as I have often said to my own children 'to be kept within these four walls'; it is a private family matter. Announcing indiscriminately to the world in general that your child was adopted is unnecessary and may indeed have a negative impact on the attachment process.

For instance, introducing your child as 'my adopted child' serves only to label a child, particularly if the child has siblings who are the biological children of the AP. While this might sound obvious, it is a commonplace occurrence in adoptive relationships. I recently read of an adult adoptee who described attending intensive therapy to help with the building of his self-esteem; a clear childhood memory was his adoptive mother's practice of introducing him as her 'adopted' son. He had an older brother who was his AP's biological son, so being designated as 'adopted' at every turn made him feel like he should have been grateful to his APs. Prior to parenthood, when I was working for the bank I previously mentioned, a client informed me that her son was adopted when there was no need to do so. The client's son was thinking of buying a house and she was planning to assist him in getting the finance. Before I even started to note down the details of the trans-action, the client informed me that her son was adopted, leading me to ponder why she felt it necessary to appraise me of such personal information or how her son might feel about his mother's openness to a stranger. Whether her son was biological or adopted had no influence on the legal or financial aspects of the transaction.

Patricia Irwin Johnson, an AP, writes that: 'Adoption is in most ways no more relevant as a lifelong label than it would be to refer to Missy as Peter's birth-control-failure daughter or to Ahmad as Bonnie's caesar-ean-section-born son. We are, and we will always be, more like families built by birth than we are unlike them' (1992, p. 205).

The pronouncement of my children's adoption has always been on a need-to-know basis. People, unaware of my adoptive parenthood, have casually commented both on lack of facial likeness between me and my children or even of a great likeness between us. I have typically just nodded in silence, not embellishing their comment with any further information. I can say with confidence that I have never introduced my children in any other way besides 'this is my son' or 'this is my daughter'.

My reticence in declaring my adoptive parenthood has led to some hilarious situations. Once while drying an eighteen-month-old Kev after a swim, a pool regular commented on how quickly he was growing. I hadn't seen this lady in a while but previously, before I had adopted Kev, we had frequently bumped into each other. 'My goodness, how time flies!' she declared. 'He's getting so big and it seems such a short time ago since I met you here pregnant with him.' I smiled and mumbled something. She had clearly convinced herself that she had seen me as a pregnant woman. My failure to correct her error made for a much-shared and much-laughed at anecdote. The guffaws were as loud at my failure to correct her mistake as for her erroneous memory of my pregnancy.

2.2. *Extended Family Attitudes to Adoption*

The claiming of children as your own is closely connected to your extended family's attitude to adoption. I have encountered APs who have decided they are no longer going to subject their children to the lack of consideration by relatives who regard the adopted children as lesser in some way: grandmothers who exclude adopted children from introductions when in family gatherings or relatives who doggedly persist in loud discussions of who is like whom (even though this is standard conversation in family gatherings), leaving the adopted child out in the cold.

Patricia Irwin Johnson writes:

> It is not unusual for APs who find certain family members or friends unwilling to consider their child one of the family, to feel strong resentments which may result in rifts. You will want to do all you can to openly discuss your concerns and your hurt feelings with this relative. While no one wants to perpetuate family rifts, the decision to distance oneself from a stubbornly unsupportive relative is a sign of a strong need to protect one's child and indicates the development of a healthy sense of entitlement between parent and child. So for several reasons, how our families feel about our children who have been adopted is important to us, as well as to the children, and it is worth our concentrated effort to facilitate those attachments (1992, p. 229).

A key aspect of making a child your own is the welcoming of them into your family circle. However, if your family circle is not a welcoming, inclusive place for your child, keeping them safely away from certain family members is equally important in making a child your own, as you are prioritising their well-being and placing it ahead of the opinions of your genetically linked family. The key aspect for APs to be aware of is the impact of possible family politics and attitudes on their children and to act to protect them accordingly, even if it means spending less time in the company of your extended family.

3. *Creating a Sanctuary to Deal with Loss*

Embracing a child's loss and providing a safe, secure haven to grieve that loss is another characteristic of attachment that applies specifically to adoption. The provision of a sanctuary by the APs to deal with loss and the acknowledgement of the child's pain and loss by the APs is key to forming a strong attachment. H. David Kirk writes that 'A clinical report suggests that the inability of adoptive parents to communicate with their children on the subject of natural parents, adversely affects the parent-child relationship' (1984, p. 96). Embracing the child's birth history can be a terrifying, daunting prospect for the AP, particularly if the history is negative or indeed absent (i.e., there is no known birth information).

However, having an ongoing adoption conversation with the adopted child is a key part of forming an attachment. When the child has a sanctuary by way of their APs in which to mull over their loss, the people within that sanctuary (the child and the APs) become closer and the bond between the APs and the child strengthens. The more you share your understanding and acceptance of their history, the closer you become to your child. The more you are open to their tears, explosive anger, tantrums and all other expressions of grief and loss, the more they will feel that their grief and loss is being acknowledged and accepted. Having our grief and loss ignored is detrimental to our well-being. If the AP refuses to accept that their child has suffered a profound loss and is unwilling to encourage their child to talk about what is really going on, then the attachment could become weak. Having your sorrow and pain validated is a powerful aid to recovery. The AP who is brave enough to encourage the child to talk about their loss of a birth family and who does not transmit the message 'Am I not enough for you?' when the child speaks about their birth family, is the AP who will securely attach. A child aware that their AP is receptive and empathic, that their grief is accepted and validated, and that their birth history is not a banned subject, will also securely attach.

While talking about adoption is not something that will be done extensively when the child is an infant, the ongoing conversation about adoption that progresses steadily as the child grows is a hugely significant part of the bonding process.

3.1. *Searching as Part of Bonding*

A lack of birth information may fuel the adopted child's imagination and turn the birth-family members into fairytale creatures. Making the birth family a reality in your child's life has a number of benefits, not least the removal of 'magical thinking' about their origins. It is essential to find out as much as possible, communicate as much as possible and make the birth family part of your relationship with your child from as early an age as possible. Once the child knows as much as there is to know about their birth family, the fantasy becomes a reality and the birth family's existence merges with the child's life.

However, this does not mean that the birth family is a physical, actual part of your family. In the case of IA, distance and language barriers will (usually) preclude contact. However, it is possible to include the names of birth family members in the ongoing conversation, and photos, if available, for the child to become familiar with. Searching for information for your child is a key contributor to bonding, and while going to the trouble and expense of employing a searcher might seem outside of the power of APs, it is an action that will reap considerable rewards in terms of solidifying the relationship.

No matter how sad, devastating or even frightening your child's story, it is uniquely theirs and must be taken on board by you. Your attitude to and respect for their birth family and history is at the core of strengthening the relationship between you and your child. It is also a key to the healthy development of your child. Sherrie Eldridge describes the bond that forms between parent and child when the grief and loss of adoption is acknowledged, and the child's birth history shared. In *Twenty Things Adopted Kids Wish Their Adoptive Parents Knew*, Eldridge introduces the image of the child nestling into their AP's arms as they grieve together for the loss of the child's birth family. This, according to Eldridge, cements a deep bond with the adopted child.

Talking to our children about their adoption and birth families will not push them away from us. However, ignoring the existence of a birth family may well do so. All of us search for our identity in some way; APs can take the view that they and their child are travellers together on a journey that is a joint search for identity. The AP is the bearer and protector of their child's birth history. The AP is the person with whom the child shares the sadness and joy of learning about who they are.

4. *Using the PLACE Model for Discipline and Bonding*

Child psychologist and author Dr Daniel Hughes (www.daniel-hughes.org) has developed the PLACE model to help children who have suffered early childhood trauma. Dr Hughes' treatment is family based and focuses on facilitating the child's ability to establish a secure attachment with their primary care-giver. He travels around the world training care professionals, and I had the pleasure of attending one of his workshops in Dublin in 2012. To establish secure attachment with their children, parents should aim to be:

Playful with the child instead of shaming them.

Loving in spite of acting out behaviour and poor choices.

Accepting of the child's thoughts, feelings and views without judgement.

Curious about the child's behaviours and reactions so the parent learns what triggers them.

Empathise about past hurts and current challenges. This is where having a sanctuary for your child to safely express loss comes in to play. The parent allows the child to grieve comfortably without judgment, dismissal or diverting of feelings.

4.1. *Disciplining my Children – I Am the 'Witch Mother'.*

The expression 'witch mother' was used by adoption counsellor and author Holly Van Gulden during a 2010 AP training workshop held in Dublin. She was describing the general parental response to challenging behaviour of children impacted by early childhood trauma. As she spoke of yelling at the child and losing the rag and acting like the 'witch mother' when boundaries were pushed and instructions ignored, I could immediately relate to her description. This was me she was talking about.

I have frequently walked a tightrope in parenting. The challenge is to try to get the balance between building self-esteem and guiding my child down the path of responsibility and accountability. An admonishment to an adopted child who has exhibited challenging behaviour borne out of insecurity and self-doubt, delivered (as it often was by me, and still is at times if I forget to check myself) with ear-piercing yells, is processed in an entirely different way to that of a birth child. The tone is read by the adopted child as: 'You hate me, you wish you hadn't adopted me. You are rejecting me just as my birth mother rejected me.' Self-evaluation, as outlined in the previous chapter, has helped me make significant improvements on my 'witch mother' tone of voice.

4.2. *Corporal Punishment – The Grey Area of Parenting*

Slapping your child is one of those topics that languishes in the grey area of parenting. There are few parents who will not admit to resorting to corporal punishment when their patience is tried in that way that only a child can do. When on the receiving end of an elaborate piece of back-chat or the repeated pushing of boundaries, my fingers have often itched to give a good sharp smack. However, the significance of my fingers itching means that, in giving in to the urge, my anger at the challenging behaviour is being vented. Instead, a disciplinary method should be deployed that is aimed at curbing such behaviour in future. Allowing your anger with your child to be discharged by inflicting violence on them as a form of punishment is not a good idea.

There is a mantra from past generations about corporal punishment: 'I got slapped at home and it never did me any harm.' Such a statement invites the question of 'How do you know it didn't do you any harm?' or even a comment of 'Just because it didn't do *you* any harm doesn't make it right.'

While corporal punishment as a means of disciplining children has been widely condemned and banned in schools since the eighties (with a universal ban in 2015), during my childhood in the sixties it was widely used. It's difficult to fathom the effect of physical discipline on children who received such treatment at the hands of concerned and well-intentioned parents. When a child acts out as a result of early childhood loss and a frazzled AP is at their wits end, physical punishment may be seen as the only option. Non-physical means of disciplining the child *is the only way*, and while that might seem like dragging out the situation with talking instead of smacking, research has shown that talking is more effective than violence in getting the message across. Slapping a child, whose self-esteem is already low as a consequence of their birth history, is *not* an option, and there is nothing grey about that.

5. *Limiting Screen Technology*

A child who has suffered early childhood loss will require extra parental input in the making, strengthening and maintaining the relationship. The AP will need to ensure that the child is not overly absorbed in a virtual world; the child should instead be aware of their actual surroundings and fully involved in their interaction with you. Screen absorption is ubiquitous – an accepted feature of modern life. However, can there be anything as sad as a young child making their way through a beautiful, tree-adorned park in the sparking sunshine, completely disengaged from their surroundings as they stare into their handheld gadget? While I am of the pre-technology era of childhood spent outside in the wilds of the Irish countryside, I know I'm not alone in pondering how much is missed out on by spending several hours a day staring at a screen.

For any parent, either biological or adoptive, the limiting of a child's time spent looking at screens will help forge a relationship. While the child is engaged in screen time (now dubbed the 'third parent'), they are not interacting with you, the parent. This is time that could be spent doing activities together such as cooking, cleaning, drawing, reading, building Lego, kicking a football, going for a walk, doing the shopping: the list is endless.

While the limiting of screens is important for any child's well-being and development, for the adopted child these limits are even more so. A child who has experienced early trauma can often be prone to reliance on 'magical thinking' as they try to make sense of their past. Submergence in the virtual world of screen technology has the potential to feed this tendency to engage in fantasy. It may lead to a child becoming over-reliant on entertainment by screens and display a reluctance to interact with real life. In *Flagging the Screenager,* Dr Harry Barry and Enda Murphy write of the emotional and social effects of screen technology on children's lives. 'One of the obvious casualties of this [excessive use of screens] can be real life friendships and relationships with family members and loved ones. These can be seen as of secondary importance to the virtual-reality world' (2014, p. 101). In a way, the limitation of screen time is another type of funnelling. This action will pay dividends as the child grows older and becomes more independent. Attachment will be to the parent and the physical world and not to the virtual world of a screen gadget.

Adopting an Older Child: Attachment

It is now widely accepted that irrespective of how young a child is when adopted, the impact of the wound of separation from their birth mother is present.

My experience of adoption is with children under the age of one. A child who has spent longer in institutional care and/or been with a number of different carers has a greater likelihood of being emotionally hurt before they reach their APs. Patricia Irwin Johnson writes: 'Older children are often victims of multiple breaks in attachment or have been attached to people who hurt them in some way and so have great difficulty learning to trust parenting figures' (1992, p. 216). Research has suggested that a child who is adopted as an infant and has spent six months or less in either institutional or foster care has a reduced chance of experiencing physical and developmental problems including difficulties with attachment, simply because they have not been exposed to the deprivations of institutional care, which include minimal staff-child interactions, absence of physical affection and educational activities (Rutter et al., 2009).

Talking about Adoption with Your Child

'The best way out is always through.' Robert Frost, 'A Servant to Servants', 1914.

Talking to your child about adoption is a conversation, not a parroting of the words 'I'm adopted' on a standalone basis. A story often told in AP circles is one regarding a three-year-old girl who was adopted and who told everyone on her first day of playschool: 'I'm a doctor.' The little girl's APs had done their best to repeat the words 'I'm adopted' to her, but the child had not understood the words or learned how to properly pronounce them.

The purpose of teaching the child to repeat the word 'adopted' is to, rightly, foster familiarisation with the word. A young child who repeats the words 'I'm adopted' will not likely understand the meaning of adoption, but at least the word will be familiar, therefore building the foundation for a more focussed conversation a year or two in the future. However, the danger is that if the word is not given some kind of context, the child will not understand, as demonstrated by the little girl in the story, where not only does she not understand what adoption means but her mispronunciation has compounded her ignorance.

Having communicated the word 'adoption', the next challenge arises when your child is able to ask, 'What is adoption?' You have to be emotionally ready to explain the facts of adoption – not necessarily your child's specific facts but the actual realities of adoption. As each stage of development arrives, your child will increase his understanding of adoption and you, the AP, must be ready to answer whatever question arises.

The Stages of the Adoption Conversation

Adoption adjustment is described by Brodzinsky et al. (1992) in *Being Adopted: The Lifelong Search for Self* as the term for two crucial processes in our life span – the search for self and the experience of loss.

Brodzinsky et al. incorporate *Erik Erikson's life-stage development model into a model of adoption adjustment. This model can also be used as a guideline for the stages of the adoption conversation. I have summarised the main points below.

Stage: Infancy

Trust vs. Mistrust. The child learns to adjust to a new (adoptive) home. They are in the process of developing secure attachment. Language learning is taking place while trust is developing. The word 'adopted' is used while talking to the infant to foster familiarisation with the word.

Stage: Toddler and Preschool Years

Autonomy vs. Shame. The child is learning about birth and reproduction as well as developing a great sense of personal control (e.g., toilet training, toy and clothing preferences). They are adjusting to the initial information about adoption via conversation about what adoption means. References to the birth family, such as repeating the birth mother's name (if known), will help the child process the existence of their other family. Initiation of the conversation at this early stage will lessen the impact of the shock of the reality of adoption during middle childhood.

Stage: Middle Childhood (Pre-Teens)

Industry vs. Inferiority: The child begins to develop a sense of pride in their accomplishments and abilities. The child is gaining an understanding of the meaning and implications of being adopted. They are searching for answers regarding their origin and relinquishment. The child may act out as a consequence of understanding the reality of adoption. The AP's readiness for conversation is vital as the child is coping with the impact of adoption: physical differences from family members, stigma associated with the relinquishment of adoption and peer's reaction to adoption. In my experience, middle childhood is the key time for mulling over birth history, regardless of whether actual information is available or not. Discussion with the child around *not knowing* anything about the birth family is as important as the imparting of whatever information is available.

Stage: Adolescence

Ego Identity vs. Identity Confusion: During adolescence, the child explores their independence and develops a sense of self. Erikson believed that if the child fails to achieve a sense of identity, role confusion results. At this stage there is further exploration into the meaning and implication of being adopted. The AP must be emotionally equipped to help the adolescent deal with adoption loss as the adolescent tries to connect their adoption to their sense of identity and considers the possibility of a search for their biological family. The AP is the source of support for any attempts to search for the birth family.

Stage: Young Adulthood

Intimacy vs. Isolation: There is further exploration of the implications of adoption as it relates to the growth of self and the development of intimacy. Further considerations of searching and of beginning the search. The AP's support and positive attitude toward the search for the birth family is vital in maintaining a strong bond.

What Adopted People Say

In the writings of adopted people, both in literature and on online forums, the scant conversation surrounding adoption during their upbringing is a recurring theme. In these writings, there is an inference that many APs observe a 'don't mention the war' policy when discussing adoption in any detail with their child. Peter F. Dodds, the German-American adoptee and author of *Outer Search, Inner Journey*, writes:

> My parents never said another word about adoption after they told me (at age 5) how they found me. Perhaps they believed it satisfied their obligation as adopted parents. I didn't want to talk about adoption because it hurt, and I was never allowed to cry or show anger. Adoption became my darkest secret, even though my parents told their adult friends (1997, p. 8).

Zara Philips writes that:

> Adoption wasn't something that was deeply discussed in the house I grew up in; it was a subject I sensed made my mother uncomfortable. I didn't know how to talk to her about it. I became the secret keeper of my true feelings, battling inwardly and quietly on the meaning of what it was to be a child who was given up for adoption (2012, p. 228).

A British-American adoptee is quoted in David M. Brodzinsky's *Being Adopted* as saying that 'When things are kept quiet and whispered about and never brought out into the open, it always takes on the aura of something awful' (1993, p. 170).

What Adoptive Parents Say

I have shared my experiences of adoptive parenthood with other APs over the years and have heard reciprocal stories and opinions. While I was in the throes of searching for birth information, one AP who had also done a lot of searching said that, from her experience, sharing your child's birth history with that child was like throwing a handful of sand into the air; the grains can land anywhere: in your eyes, in your clothes, or just fly away on the breeze. The child's reaction is unpredictable. You can never know if you did the right thing by telling or if you conveyed the story in a sensitive way.

Another AP said she would be terrified of searching for fear of what she would find and that she avoided talking about adoption with her children as the mention of their adoption reminded her that she was unable to give birth, and that reminder was like a knife through her heart.

The Reluctance to Talk about Adoption

The cauldron of emotions at the heart of adoption makes for a topic of interest. Given that close to 50,000 people in Ireland have been adopted (Adoption Authority of Ireland Annual Report, 2016) and when the numbers touched by adoption are considered, an extensive portion of the population is impacted by adoption. In Ireland, however, adoption as a topic has not been widely discussed, analysed or researched. Yes, we have myriad adoption 'stories' that illustrate how adoption embodies everything that is fundamental to being human, including the search for identity. Apart from outlining how individual adoption experiences pan out, adoption as a process has rarely been openly and comprehensively examined through the lens of loss and grief.

In many ways, talking to your child about adoption is like having the sex-education conversation: we know we must have the conversation, but we put it off as we are unsure of how good a job we'll make of it or how we will deal with the reactions and questions. As previously mentioned, our reluctance to raise the topic of adoption with our child stems from the fear of evocation of our own losses, a reminder of what we were unable to do, bringing back the trauma and disappointment of our infertility, which compounds our reluctance to raise the topic with our child. It also brings up the losses experienced by the adopted child.

The Terror of Being Hurt

Joe Soll, adoptee and author, speaks about fear in his YouTube video 'Terror is Non-Negotiable' (see www.adoptionhealing.com/terror). Soll says that the terror of being hurt prevents us from revealing our true feelings. 'Why do so many adoptees and moms have so many walls up? Does it mean that they don't care? Is their behaviour disrespectful? I believe the answer to all this is terror, non-negotiable terror'. Soll refers to birth mothers and adopted people in his video, but the same fear can be attributed to APs, which can result in APs avoiding the topic of adoption.

The complexity of adoption is never more palpable than when talking about it to our child. No matter how much or how little birth information there is surrounding the child, having the adoption conversation is a test of any AP's mettle.

The Rules of Telling – The Best Way Out Is Through

I have summarised the rules of telling below. These rules are taken from Keefer and Schooler, *Telling the Truth to Your Adopted or Foster Child: Making Sense of the Past*, 2000, pp. 87–96).

1. Open the conversation about adoption. Your initiation is the cornerstone of the adoption conversation. Children often believe they are being disloyal to the adoptive family when they have feelings and questions about their birth family and, consequently, they may avoid the topic, even if they have questions or troubling feelings. APs must look for opportunities to raise the issue of adoption and ask the child for questions. The child must see that the door is always open as far as discussing adoption is concerned.

2. Use positive adoption language at all times. Use the phrase 'birth' parents rather than 'real' or 'natural' parents (although the latter expressions are commonly used where adoption is discussed by the media). The use of the words 'real' or 'natural' may lead the child, while they are young, to question the validity of adoptive parenthood and the substantiality of the relationship with their AP. Use my 'child/son/daughter' rather than my 'adopted child/son/daughter' when introducing your child to others. A child who is constantly referred to as 'adopted' sees the term as a label that marks them out from other children who are biological.

3. Never lie to a child about any aspect of their birth history. Keefer and Schooler warn that if an AP chooses to lie to their child and the truth is later revealed by a family associate or the child discovers adoption-related documents, a serious rift in the parent/child relationship occurs, a rift which is difficult to repair with an apology or

explanation. Children are often more troubled by a lack of honesty on the part of their APs rather than by the actual information received.

4. Allow a child to express anger toward a birth family member without joining in. No matter how negatively the birth parent is presented through the birth story, the AP cannot allow the indulgence of speaking negatively of the birth family. This might be an easy concept to grasp, Keefer and Schooler tell us, but a difficult task to accomplish, especially when the AP is angry at birth-family members who might have harmed their children.

5. Omissions are okay until age twelve, advise Keefer and Schooler. After that, *all* information must be shared. The complete story may be too complicated or too 'adult' to share with a young child. The child's developmental level and understanding should be taken into consideration, irrespective of age, and the AP is the person in the best position to make the decision to share a birth story. Almost all teenagers, unless developmentally delayed, have the cognitive skills and sophistication to understand their history.

6. Keefer and Schooler say that if the information is negative, use a third party such as a suitably qualified psychotherapist to help with the imparting of a difficult birth history. There is an old saying about 'shooting the messenger' that applies in the case of sharing extremely negative information about the birth family. A post-adoption specialist helps the AP to avoid becoming the messenger.

7. Don't try to 'repair' the pain of adoption. Naturally, parents try to protect their children from pain. However, APs have to recognise that their child must experience some pain in the normal resolution of adoption-related grief. The best way out is through. It is unrealistic to expect that APs can, by saying exactly the right thing, erase all of the pain and sadness caused by the separation from the birth family. 'Sometimes, in the parental eagerness to take pain away from our children, we instead take away the validity of their feelings' (Keefer and Schooler, 2000, p. 93). We all have our own experiences of others offering platitudes when we suffer a loss or disappointment: 'It could be worse, at least you still have your health' or 'It was a happy release for her – it's better that she's no longer suffering'. These are not helpful. My daughter has spoken of

feeling overwhelmed with grief when she thinks of her birth family. It has always been a challenge for me not to respond by saying that she is better off now that she is surrounded by a loving family. Instead, I respond that separation from her birth family must be very hard for her and it is natural that she feels overwhelmingly sad.

8. A child should have control over telling their story outside of the immediate family, say Keefer and Schooler. Remember that the birth story belongs to the child, not to the APs. If extended family or friends look for sensitive information, simply tell them that the information belongs to the child and that you are leaving it for them to share, if and when they want to. Let the child know that they are not keeping information to themselves because it is shameful, but because they should not have to explain their private history in all its detail to anyone and everyone.

Finding the Right Moment

There always seems to be something else more important to do, and few opportune moments in the fast pace of life for deeply personal, intense conversations with your child. Finding a safe place for intimate conversation is not easy. An AP once declared to me (when I was sharing with him my own experience of the adoption conversation) that you cannot 'sit a three-year-old down and tell him he was adopted'. I agree. The goal of the AP is to ensure their child feels as if they have always known they were adopted, that there was never one day when their APs had to 'sit him down and tell him he was adopted'.

For me, there were a few key ways I introduced the adoption conversation:

At Bedtime

If your family is religious, saying a short, simple prayer before bedtime is an appropriate way of referring to the birth family without the necessity of having a deep conversation. From when both of my children were infants, I recited a prayer that included the members of the birth family. This ritual happened from when they were as young as two – in

Tatiana's case, a year old. By the time they both decided that observing religious rituals was not of huge importance to them anymore, they had processed the reality of their birth history and no longer needed to parrot a night-time prayer for their birth family.

Bedtime is not the ideal or recommended time for *opening up* the adoption conversation, as reference to this may well cause occasional sleeplessness (as both of my children have suffered from over the years as a result of me opening up the adoption conversation at bedtime). Nevertheless, the nightly reference to their birth family created a solid base for the adoption conversation, which I then continued to mention at opportune times during the day when either child was alone with me. Creating a familiarity with the names of their birth family allowed for an easy opening of the conversation with them.

By Sharing Other Adoption Stories:

As each child grew older and praying at night lessened, sharing other adopted people's stories was a way to start a general dialogue without an immediate, direct focus on 'self'. Anyone who has an interest in adoption literature, whether blogs, books or articles, will know there's an abundance of riches as far as stories about adoption experiences are concerned. Every human being has a unique story, and those who have shared their story have contributed greatly to helping others understand the struggle. Talking about another adopted person's struggles served to keep the topic centred on someone else while still talking about adoption. Often, I shared details of stories I had read, and my children's reaction to those stories helped to get a conversation going. Again, each child was alone with me when I told the story, as being on my own with either one of them ensured intimacy and privacy.

A story I shared with Kev at age sixteen was about an adopted person who found out she was adopted when she was in her forties. To the woman's abject dismay, her parents had never told her she was adopted. She described the betrayal and hurt she felt about being, as she called it, 'lied to all her life'. Kev reacted strongly to the story, describing in clear terms how angry he would be if his adoption had been kept secret from him. Hearing about another person's challenges allowed him to comment and release emotion on the subject.

It also meant he could compare himself with someone else in a similar position. Recounting other adopted people's stories has been a way for me, throughout the years, to get Kev and Tatiana talking about their feelings on adoption.

By Making Sure It Was Just the Two of Us

Being alone with either child, away from the family home, presents opportunities for intimate conversation. The change of location can foster a fresh perspective on the life events teased out in the discussion. While Tatiana and I had lunch together last summer in a noisy café in Piccadilly, London, surrounded by strangers, she spoke at length about her birth family in Kazakhstan and her hopes for future reconnection.

The Fear of Appearing Ungrateful

Adopted people often say that they were unable to express their grief or consider searching for their birth family because of a fear of appearing ungrateful to their APs. Fear of hurting the AP is a common theme that runs throughout the writings of adopted people. This fear would explain why many adopted people wait until the AP is dead before searching for their birth family. This reduces the chances of a successful reunion due to the possible death of the birth parents by that time. APs who have fully accepted the reality of adoption will understand that their child is doing something natural and necessary in searching for their birth family and must convey this to the adopted child.

Dealing with Loss

The acknowledgement of the existence of a loss helps to lessen that loss. Having the adoption conversation is a step in the direction of lessening a loss. When loss is unacknowledged and silence reigns, then the loss festers and multiplies. When loss is lifted out and given a good shake, stared at, questioned, reflected on, justified and treated with the respect it deserves, then the loss becomes much less of an influence on life. It remains, but in a much more manageable way. Sherrie Eldridge

(1999) writes that loss and grief need to be verbalised and that APs who are in denial of this add another trauma to what the child has already suffered. Eldridge states that the adopted child must grieve their loss if they are to fully receive love in the future.

The trauma of separation from the birth mother followed by child-hood in institutional care has been shown to foster attachment disorder and learning difficulties (Rutter et al., 2009). A 2017 report on IA in the ICGP journal *Forum* stated that due to the specialist nature of the care needs of adopted children, GPs are susceptible to lacking educa-tion and knowledge of these issues. There is evidence of high levels of diagnosis of ADHD amongst adopted children. Keefer and Schooler write that:

> It is likely that adopted and foster children are sometimes mistakenly diagnosed as having ADD, ADHD, or other learning disorders because they are *preoccupied* with the emotional work of resolving loss, identity development, anger, lack of trust, and so on. Such preoccupation gets in the way of learning because it funnels the child's available energy and attention away from the cognitive domain, the learning domain, of human development. Instead of placing angry, frightened, insecure children in time-out, we need to place them with counsellors, therapists, and/ or support groups that address their issues and allow them to concentrate and engage in learning (2000, p. 220).

Where parents are able to engage in the adoption conversation with their child and consequently help the child to absorb and understand the loss of adoption, many bad behaviours directly triggered by loss may well be helped. It is one thing to talk to your child briefly and without elaboration about their adoption, and a whole other thing to carry on the conversation, exploring it all, answering the questions, encouraging reflection and helping with the child's pain.

If the child gets the sense that their questions make their APs uncomfortable, then they will not ask. Instead, they will bottle up their feelings and act out or retreat. Also, it is likely that children whose heads are full with adoption-related anxieties are often unable to cope with learning in school. Keefer and Schooler write of the adopted child's preoccupation with emotional loss which gets in the way of learning 'because it funnels the child's available energy and attention away from the cognitive domain, the learning domain, of human development' (p. 220).

I would take this a step further and say that the AP's emotional ability to carry on the adoption conversation might prove to be in direct correlation with the development of the child's emotional stability. The AP's fear and reluctance to discuss adoption with the child is mirrored in the child's ability to face the challenges of life. The ability of the AP to sustain the adoption conversation is, therefore, one of the most intrinsically important aspects of rearing an emotionally well-adjusted adopted child. The more closed-off the AP is with their willingness or tenacity in opening discussion about the child's birth origins, the more likely the child is to exhibit loss-related behaviours.

Adoptees Have the Least Choice

'Adoptees don't really have rights, their lives are about supporting the secrets, the needs and desires of others.' A. M. Homes (2007, p. 20).

Of the three parties who are chiefly involved in adoption, the adoptee has the least choice in what happens. Of the three parties, the AP has the most power to obtain, on behalf of their child, the most precious and vital component for self-actualisation: the child's birth information. Including the birth history in the rearing of a child is a challenge. APs need help and support with communicating the challenging birth history to their child in an age-appropriate way. The AP is in prime position to assist the adopted child deal with issues of loss and to help her child with search and reunion, and so their role is complex. Not only is it about nurturing the child, but it is also about the AP personally processing the child's history and communicating that history in a way that allows the child to develop a sturdy self-image. The adoptee has the least choice in their adoption, but by connecting the adoptee with their birth history, the AP goes some way toward alleviating the impact of that lack of choice. Having the adoption conversation in a sensitive, age-appropriate and timely way is one of the greatest contributors to the child's development and general well-being.

Available Birth Information

An essential aspect of talking about adoption with your child is the use of available birth information. In the case of IA, birth history is often minimal or worse still, as has been reported in some adoptions, falsified. The latter is a potential nightmare for the adoptive family. Having basic information such as the birth mother's name or siblings (if any) helps in the communicating of the adoption story. Despite the attendant sadness for the child, APs often find it easier if there is no information at all. Betty Jean Lifton writes:

> I was amazed at the number of adoptive parents who seem relieved to know as little as possible. One woman said: 'I deliberately learned *nothing,* so I won't be lying to my daughter when I say I don't know the answers to her questions.' I was to discover from my questionnaires and interviews with adoptive parents how prevalent this *know as little as possible* attitude is. In answer to a later question – what they hoped for their children – these same parents were unanimous in replying that they wanted them to lead happy lives, be successful in their work and secure in themselves. They did not understand that the lack of knowledge of their heritage might be the very stumbling block to their children becoming those mature, trusting, well-adjusted adults in the future: that if their past was an 'anonymous thing,' their children could well become anonymous people' (1988, pp. 194–195).

There may be comfort in not knowing how your child came to be with you. The comfort of not knowing may deplete once the adopted child reaches adolescence. As a child grows, the challenges of life increase anyway. Brodzinsky (1992) writes about the additional challenges for the adopted adolescent as they cope with peer reaction to adoption, connecting adoption to their sense of identity, and coping with racial identity. The absence of birth information, while painful for the adopted teenager, is not an excuse for silence on the topic of adoption. Irrespective of how little is known by way of birth information, the conversation with your child must take place. Having birth information is not a pre-requisite for talking to the child about adoption. The adoption conversation must happen whether birth information is available or not. The conversation is not necessarily about what is known about the child's history but about how they perceive the lack of information (if that is the case) and how that is impacting on them.

Conclusion

The significance of the adoption conversation and its impact on the parent-child relationship is accurately described by Betty Lifton:

> Listen well – I am talking about exorcism. These conversations will undoubtedly lead to the primal questions about birth and birth parents. Adoptive parents should be prepared for them and stop at nothing to provide their children with the answers they need – yes, including their birth names – even if it means going back to agencies, calling doctors or lawyers, petitioning the court, or travelling to the child's country of origin. Rather than lose a child, they will keep one (1988, p. 276).

*Erik Erikson's life stage development model: As the individual develops, society places new demands on them and each new demand provokes an emotional crisis, the resolution of which leads to the development of a new 'virtue' or 'vital strength' (Sugarman, 2001).

Chapter Seven

SEARCH AND REUNION – A BLOOD TRAIL

'Adoptees cannot truly claim their adoptive mothers and
fathers until they have claimed themselves and the people
from whom they spring.'

Betty Lifton, *Lost and Found*

'Reunions often seem to have a calming effect . . . as if the
adoptee had been holding his breath for all those years and
could begin breathing again. There is a release of tension
and renewal of life.'

Nancy Newton Verrier,
The Primal Wound: Understanding the Adopted Child

Search and Reunion is a momentous step. For the AP, the communication of birth history can be daunting enough to contemplate and
negotiate, but the very concept of searching for and setting up contact
with their child's birth family can rattle the bravest of APs, even though,
overwhelmingly, adoption writing emphasises the importance of birth-
family connection. While search and reunion in adoption usually relates
to the adopted person's endeavours to search for and reunite with their
birth family, the account outlined here relates to a search undertaken
by me, the AP.

Each Birth Story is Unique

'The first thing you as an adoptive parent must do is face your greatest
fear, which is being rejected by your child. You may envision your child
reuniting with his birth parents someday and then wanting nothing

more to do with you. The truth is, what is likely to happen at reunion is just the opposite of what you fear.' Sherrie Eldridge (1999, p. 101).

Every family is different. Every child's birth history is different. Adoptees' individual stories are as varied and complex as life itself. While adoption is permeated with loss, in the case of where birth parents faced grim challenges leading up to the relinquishment of their baby, the adoptee, in turn, faces the prospect of an additional loss: hearing and processing their painful birth story. Nowadays, the prime driver of modern day relinquishment of an infant is economic deprivation. Birth parent neglect, abuse or substance misuse may be the reason why a child is placed for adoption (Howe, 2009). In the past, particularly in Ireland, adoption was linked to the 'taboo' of single motherhood when a woman was forced to relinquish her child due to religious and societal pressures.

As relinquishment at birth is loss imbued, it follows that many birth stories are painful, both for the AP to communicate and for the child to process. The details of the child's birth circumstances may or may not be available at the time of adoption. The documentation accompanying the adoption papers will include whatever birth information was given by the birth mother when the child was placed up for adoption. This information may include: the birth mother's name, age, address, occupation, name of birth father, details of siblings, phone number and circumstances surrounding relinquishment, e.g., economic hardship. The amount of available information at the time of the child's adoption is a key contributor to the success of the search, when and if it is eventually undertaken.

In other cases, there may be birth information, but it might have been falsified by a desperate birth mother who has tried to cover her tracks as a result of societal or family pressures. This presents an extremely difficult scenario, as having information in the first place offers hope to an adoptee desperately searching for birth relatives, only to have that hope dashed when a search reaches a dead end as a result of falsified details.

In many cases, there is no birth information at all. This can be the case if the child was abandoned (without identifying information) due to prevailing laws or cultural pressures. This can be the most challenging of all, as there is no chance of the adoptee obtaining detailed birth information and very slim prospects of a birth family reunion.

As stated in the previous chapter, no matter how apparently straightforward the information, incorporating the story of a child's birth history into their rearing is one of the most challenging aspects of adoptive parenthood.

The Need to Search

'Your child needs to be free to pursue his search without worrying about making you comfortable and secure' Sherrie Eldridge (1999, p. 207).

While the search is a common theme throughout adoptee writings, equally as common a theme is that of adoptees not wishing to hurt their APs by searching for their birth family. The implication is that seeking out their birth parents is a bad idea as far as APs are concerned.

During the summer of 2013, Averil Power, former Irish Senator, spoke about meeting her birth mother. During the interview aired on RTÉ Radio One, Averil referred to her APs and her worry that they would be hurt by her desire to search for her birth history. The AP's discomfort with their child's primal and natural need to know their birth family is something that can be helped by self-evaluation. As APs, we must accept our children's need to know their birth history. While all children, whether adopted or not, are 'borrowed' (only with us until they are ready to head into the world), the difference for APs is that there is another set of parents out there and/or an extended family who carries our beloved child's genes. The need for the child to make some sort of connection with their birth family, however tenuous, is a fundamental need no AP can ignore. The connection can be as tenuous as having a photograph, or even just discovering the details of the birth family tree. Any of these tenuous connections are likely to be enough to satisfy a child's need to know and will later be followed by bigger decisions regarding reunion once adulthood has been reached.

To want to see yourself in others is natural. This is most prevalent in IA where adopted people have spoken of their longing to interact with others who look like them. The term 'genealogical bewilderment' is used by British researcher H. J. Sants in 1964 and cited in Brodzinsky (1992) to describe a sense of disconnectedness, a feeling of being cut off from your heritage, your culture and your race.

Brodzinsky writes that the feelings of belonging and security are nurtured by looking like the people around you. The establishment of a connection with the birth family, no matter how small, depends on the circumstances of individual adoptions. The connection may be as slight as just knowing a birth mother's name or as solid as establishing regular contact, leading eventually to a face-to-face reunion.

Whatever the circumstances, support and empathy, with or without available birth information, must be provided by the AP whose door should always be open for the adoption conversation and who should be prepared for wherever that conversation might lead.

A Search Does Not Always Mean a Reunion

Search and reunion can be two very different parts of adoption, particularly in IA. In IA, physical distance and language barriers impede reunions but searching for the birth family on behalf of your child with the help of a professional searcher is common practice. Initially, it may be enough to employ an international searcher to locate birth-family information for your child and keep this information in trust for them. Gradually, in an age-appropriate way, the information can be communicated, and when they are old enough they can then decide if they want to have a reunion.

Joyce Maguire Pavao makes the distinction between search and reunion in her 2005 book, *The Family of Adoption:*

> 'Finding the information that will be the truth for that child and as parents, to convey it in ways that make sense to their child at his particular developmental stage. This is the search – all the questioning that leads up to finding the birth family. The reunion is the actual meeting … remember, a search is not always a reunion' (2005, p. 111).

It is possible to search for your child's birth information and hold it in trust for them until they are old enough to be told the details and afterwards for them to have it in their possession until they are ready to take a step toward reunion. Deciding how much and when to tell your child in an age-appropriate way is a challenging task and one you can approach with the support of an adoption professional. The search is the first step, and one that can long precede any decision to reunite with the birth family. A tenuous connection may well be enough to help your child. The emotional pressure of reunion means that an actual meeting is best left until they are an adult, i.e. over eighteen years old. The general guidance from post-adoption support services says that reunion should take place either *before* middle childhood, that is, age nine to eleven years, or, failing that, in late adolescence/early adulthood, that is age eighteen and over. In between lies all the turmoil of the teen years, the finding of self and the 'ego identity versus identity confusion', as described by Erik Erikson.

In my opinion, a teenager already trying to survive the shark-infested waters of modern life, such as peer and exam pressure, relationships and concerns about body image, identity and physical appearance, is likely to struggle with the additional complications of a birth family reunion. Therefore, I am suggesting that any steps toward reunion, if they haven't been made pre-teen, are best left until the child has reached adulthood.

Why Would an Adoptive Parent Search?

'Post-adoption contact can, and often does, present emotional challenges to adoptive parents and birth relatives.' E. Neil, *International Advances in Adoption Research for Practice* (2009, p. 287).

APs searching for information on behalf of their children has not traditionally been a common occurrence. E. Wayne Carp writes that: 'Given the social and psychological pressures discouraging contact between adoptees and birth family, it is not surprising that only 15 percent of all adoptive parents contacted the society [who arranged the adoption] for help with tracing birth information' (1998, p. 75). Given that Carp's writing is now eighteen years old, I estimate that currently, a much higher percentage of APs have attempted to trace birth information on behalf of their adopted child.

All humans want to know their roots, all humans are curious about where they sprung from – hell, I was curious to see what my children's birth family looked like, so why wouldn't *they* be curious too? In the early days of my adopting Kev in the late nineties, much negative publicity dominated IA in the news. IA placed a child at an insurmountable distance from their birth family and birth culture, severing them completely from their roots, and this was the main reason for the attack against it. Back then, in the early nineties, when I read what seemed like a never-ending stream of invective towards APs who separated children from their roots, images of Kev's family in Russia swam in my head, planting the early seeds of determination to connect with them.

My search for birth information has also been driven by the ocean of writing by adopted people about the loss they experienced. Thanks to the bravery and honesty of people who have written about their adoption loss and the lack of opportunities for contact with their internationally distant birth family, those of us who can do something to help someone else have been able to do so. An interesting exercise has been the 'What if?' scenario, which helped me cultivate empathy toward my children and their need to connect with their birth family. Any AP can try this out. What if I, Mari Gallagher, Irish woman, were to wake up aged eight months in a small town in deepest Siberia, having been adopted by a Russian couple, transported from my native County Leitrim and destined never to know my beloved mother, father, sister, brothers, cousins, aunts, uncles, in order to be raised as a Russian woman? What if I, Mari Gallagher, were to have my name changed to a Russian name, with all my Irish-ness wiped away with my new identity? My initial reaction to this scenario is to feel a lump of ice in the pit of my stomach. Notwithstanding my commitment, like any other mother, to rearing my children to the utmost of my ability, the unalterable fact remains that no matter how hard I work at my parenting, my children have had a major part of their identity taken from them. If it were me in their shoes, I have no doubt that I would grieve. The very least I would feel I deserved was my AP's help to assist me in recovering the chunk of my identity removed by adoption.

Searching for the Birth Family of an Internationally Adopted Child

In the aftermath of adopting my children, it never occurred to me that it was possible to search for further birth information early in their childhood, that is, before the landmark age of eighteen. The adoption documentation included basics on their birth family – names, dates of birth, addresses, occupations and numbers of siblings. At the time of each adoption, my emotions were on a high during my stay in each country and I barely scanned the birth family information. When I departed Russia and Kazakhstan with my child in my arms, I closed a door on those countries. The size and diversity of both countries formed a barrier in my head, forbidding me to contemplate re-negotiating their terrain, at least until the children were much older. The Russian judge who signed off on Kev's adoption papers was emphatic that we were to keep the 'secret' of adoption, a stern order delivered in a firm, peremptory tone that implied no further contact. Distance and language difference were both physical barriers to communication. Search and reunion was a hazy, indefinite possibility somewhere in the dim, distant future when the children had reached adulthood.

Even though I was resolute in keeping the adoption conversation going, I hadn't ever thought about taking a step further and conducting an actual search so early on in the children's lives. As previously mentioned, I had included their birth families' names (which had fortunately been included in the adoption documents from each country) in our nightly prayers, so their birth families had an implicit reality in our lives.

The Shock of Possible Birth Family Contact

Until a chance conversation with another AP who had herself employed a searcher, I was happy enough just to say a prayer with my children for these elusive people – almost like praying for long-deceased relatives. An actual, physical search for those frequently mentioned-in-prayers birth family members had not occurred to me. It was easy talking about people who were not actually present. In a way, by praying for them with Kev and Tatiana, I was engaging in a type of fairy story. I was talking about mythical people who only existed in a sort of virtual world thousands of miles away, a world that would not likely ever collide with mine. I was happy enough to talk about my children's birth families as long as I didn't have to encounter them.

I can still remember the jolt when the AP whom I met up with described receiving a pile of documents from Russia as a result of her search – photos of a birth mother taken by a searcher at a meeting, addresses, a letter from the birth mother and a detailed report of the birth family history. My response was 'But can you do that?'

Dread settled over me, mixed with excitement as the possibility of facing reality hit me – actually making contact with people I had been talking about for years. The AP assured me that a number of Irish APs had conducted successful searches. Because my children's birth families lived thousands of miles away, there was safety in the cocoon of unknowing. I was acknowledging their indisputable presence without ever having to experience the reality of their existence. Realising that I could actually make contact with them, learn more about them, that they could actually become real and influential people, was a shock to my system.

Life Expectancy

While life expectancy rates in both Russia and Kazakhstan have improved in the last decade, the figures have been bleak in the past. When the children were just out of their toddler years, I envisioned that by the time they began a search (if they did one) for their birth history, there was a strong chance that the birth parents might not still be around, which would remove the opportunity for a reunion. This reality further drove my resolve to obtain as much information as possible while everyone involved was still likely to be alive.

My Personal Story

As a couple with a small extended family unit, there was greater freedom to search for our children's birth families. We didn't have to be on high-alert to the possible sensitivities of family who lived nearby because (a) we would probably have had to keep secret our intention to search, which in itself would be pressurising due to the amount of time it took up and (b) when they found out they might worry that their familial positions were going to be impacted by potentially new, more influential family members. There is a vast difference between APs who are themselves parentless and living a distance from their siblings, as we were, and APs who have a large, close-knit family nearby. My own personal history was the key driver in the decision to search.

When my parents died (within a year of each other) in the early nineties, I was cut adrift. All the domestic aspects of my life had to be rearranged. Where was my home now? The house I had been reared in no longer had the security and hospitality of parental presence. In a way, my life had to be completely restructured. The isolation and feeling of rootlessness I experienced in the years following their deaths gave me a sense of what it must be like to be orphaned or separated from your natural parents. Even though, in contrast to adopted people, I had the comfort of birth parents in my life for thirty years, the upheaval of my loss was still stark and left an acutely painful mark.

My experience of losing both my parents when I was just thirty years old informed my attitude to search and reunion. How could the adopted person *not* want to discover their origins? How could the adopted person *not* crave to connect with someone who has the same blood line? This craving to know was apparent in my children from the start. I sensed they understood their loss and had experienced a deep wound. As the person closest to them, I was aware of their reactions, expressions and behavioural patterns. On the other hand, the very aspect of being without parental influence, while leaving me bereft, gave me free reign in the hunting down of my children's birth information.

My Children's Birth Family Are My Extended Family

Adoption can be viewed in the same light as marriage. In marriage, like adoption, two people are connected by love and law, there is no blood link. In a happy, successful marriage, your spouse is your best friend, your next of kin and the closest person to you.

In making a spouse a part of our lives, we also take his/her family. It's the real case of 'love me, love my dog'. The entourage of in-laws: parents, siblings, cousins, aunts and uncles, have joined us for better or worse, for richer or poorer. Central to the success of the marriage is the outcome of each spouse's efforts to get along with their respective in-laws. Whatever the relationship, there is one thing a spouse certainly cannot do – ignore the existence of the in-laws. They are an intrinsic part of your partner, for better or worse, till death do you part. The birth family of our child is, in many ways, the equivalent of the in-laws.

Irrespective of lack of information, birth parents have existed and may (more than likely) still exist. We cannot, as APs, walk away from this fact. Secrecy and lack of information is a feature of (most) closed adoptions. If the child has been born and abandoned in a foreign country without any identifying information, then the chances of contact are slim. Our adopted children did not just make themselves. It is an incontrovertible fact that a man and a woman made a child together and the woman gave birth. Just because the birth family are not physically evident in our lives does not mean they are not present. The protection of the birth mother's 'secret' has always been paramount. The birth mother walks away and gets on with her life. She has given birth, but it is a secret. An obtuse approach protects this so-called secret, but this infant will grow into an adult who will need to know about their birth history. They will not be an accepting infant forever. This secrecy is also bolstered by the feelings of APs toward parenthood. Making a child our own is an essential part of the bonding process, but in that bonding process, there must also be the recognition of other people who are deeply connected to the child. Our new adopted in-laws, as it were.

When I set out on my journey of adoptive parenthood, the existence of another family in my child's life was a reality I did not initially dwell on. If I was to think deeply about them, then they would become real people experiencing real losses and would thus dilute my determination as I completed the journey of becoming an AP. It took time to accept that my children's birth family were part of my family.

Preventative Health Strategy

'Empathic orientation towards the child's natural parents thus implies a preliminary "acknowledgement of difference" by adoptive parents. By such orientation, the original parents enter the constellation of the new family.' H. David Kirk, *Shared Fate* (1984, p. 70).

The expression 'preventative health strategy' was used in Betty J. Lifton's *Lost and Found*. Birth parents who were trying to make contact with their child wrote the following in a letter to the AP: 'We're recommending a preventative health strategy now in Debbie's [the adopted child] early teens. It'll be a lot harder later' (1988, p. 251). Preventative health strategy evokes the saying 'prevention is better than cure'. Lifton was advocating early contact with birth parents to ensure the adopted child would enter adulthood accepting their adoption instead of being consumed with the need to search.

While I do not have experience of being contacted by birth parents – what happened in my case was the other way around – I do agree with the concept of 'preventative health strategy'. If it is possible to help the child early on by providing tenuous contact with the birth family, (not necessarily physical contact as advocated by Lifton) then there's no reason not to try. Tenuous contact would be incorporating the birth family into the child's life in some way, whether just by photographs or a birth story, from as early an age as possible, was my attempt at a preventative health strategy. As dealt with in the previous chapter, the suppression of the natural desire of the child to talk about their birth family has deep-seated affects.

Adoption – Closed or Open?

Closed Adoption

Adoption, as far as I was concerned, was a closure of the relationship between the birth family and the child. While the word 'closed' suggested a grim finality, I initially accepted closed adoption as part and parcel of the deal. The birth mother disappeared from the child's life and left the APs to get on with the rearing of the child until the child grew to adulthood and decided to search if they wished. In the early days of adoptive parenting, I only thought of my role as a parent; the concept of my child potentially *needing* birth contact had not entered my understanding.

Years later, when I found Kev's birth relatives on social media, I consulted with a post-adoption support service about what to do next. The reply was: 'You would be opening up the adoption if you initiate contact with the birth family'. Those words, 'opening up the adoption', raised all sorts of images for me, the main one being Pandora opening up her mythical box and releasing myriad dark, wispy spirits into the air.

By opening up the adoption, I was changing the game, rearranging the landscape around the contract of adoption and maybe even breaching it. Musing on whether to 'open up the adoption' led me back to that afternoon a decade previously in the courtroom in Nizhny Tagil, Russia, when the judge made us pledge to keep the 'secret of adoption'. By ignoring this exhortation and initiating contact with the birth family, I was unearthing the 'secret of adoption' and in the best interest of my child, breaking the promises made in the courtroom, cutting through the fear, facing reality and taking a risk. While considering the search, I connected with an online US-based adoptive parent group who had made contact with birth families in several countries including Russia. Searching for birth families, despite the apparent strictness of the 'keep the secret of adoption' exhortation, was happening on a large scale.

At the time of writing, our adoption arrangement with both birth families is semi-open, in that an actual physical meeting has not taken place. However, contact is in place, and should either child wish in the future to take this contact into a physical meeting (something I believe with certainty will happen), then the groundwork has been done.

Open Adoption

Open adoption is officially defined as an arrangement where the birth parents meet the APs and an agreement is made about ongoing meetings between the child and the birth parents. Betty Lifton (1988) defines open adoption as 'cooperative adoption' – a process where the birth parents and APs meet and exchange identifying information. Lifton also asks the question: 'How open is open?' and ponders if the adoption is open 'just a crack' – semi-open – where the birth parents and APs may exchange pictures and letters without meeting. Making contact with the birth family and setting up ongoing communication is opening the adoption 'just a crack', as described by Lifton.

Martha M. Ertman (2015) writes about contracts and the bad press they receive, when in fact, contracts shape and sustain families, none more so than in the case of adoptive families. The closed adoption is the most commonplace arrangement in adoption, where there is zero contact with the birth parents and the birth information may or may not be available. Ertman points out that years of experience shared by adopted people indicates the importance of making adoption as open as is comfortable for the parties concerned.

Ertman writes of the long-term benefits to adoptive and birth families of open adoption arrangements. She cites adoption researchers H. Grotevant and Ruth McRoy's (1998) study of open adoption, which suggests that such arrangements often involve 'more pain upfront', ('upfront' meaning 'at a younger age') but in three or four years the children, APs and birth parents are 'much more settled' than in closed adoptions. Because the child learns early in their life of the circumstances of their birth, and in many cases has monitored contact with their birth family, the pain of loss is experienced while they are still young (hence the expression 'more pain upfront'), making the acceptance of their adoption more likely as they grow toward adulthood.

Ertman includes a range of contracts for all kinds of relationships, not just adoptive. She outlines the benefits of being upfront about domestic and personal arrangements. For example, in the case of an unmarried couple living together, she outlines a 'Sample Cohabitation Agreement', which includes pledges to agree to counselling sessions before ending the relationship and ways in which income and property will be shared. Her sample 'Open Adoption Agreement', to be signed by both the birth parent and the AP, contains many sentiments I believe are integral to adoption:

> Together we give this child the great necessities of life: the roots of security and wings of opportunity. With hope in our hearts, we collectively offer a blend of security and nurture. It was love for children in general that put us on converging paths, and now it is our love for this unique child that unites us for the shared journey ahead.
>
> We stand committed to our ideals. We believe that children have innate dignity. We are convinced that children are not possessions to be hoarded but rather gifts from God to be selflessly loved. We believe that children need security and stability, and we recognize that they innocently depend on the adults in their lives for these comforts We believe relationships thrive in an atmosphere of honesty and mutual respect. We recognize that

if any one of us is diminished, we all are. Therefore we pledge to centre on the child and elevate his or her interest above our own, be honest in our interactions, take time to consider situations from the perspectives of others, convey newly discovered medical information, consider mediation in the event of major misunderstanding or disagreement, send the birth parent letters and pictures once a month and arrange for visits on special occasions as well as phone contact on a regular basis (pp. 204–205).

Attitudes and Reactions to Search and Reunion

The following are reactions of APs upon hearing of another AP instigating a search for their adopted child's birth information:

'Better keep negative news from them [adopted children] until they are late into their teens and can understand.'

'If I told my adopted child she has a birth sibling, my biological child would get jealous and confused.'

'My child has enough problems without having to deal with hearing about the birth family.'

'My child never asks anything about adoption, so why should I even broach the subject?'

'We make very little of their adoption, hardly talk about it at all, we reckon it's better that way.'

When I spoke of my experience of searching for the birth family on behalf of my children, many APs verbalised my own fears and doubts. They asked why I would do such a thing. Was I not potentially causing trouble for the birth mother by sending a strange man (the international searcher) looking for her? Was I not drawing attention to her and the past she may well be trying to keep secret? These were valid points and such worries have stayed with me. However, the reason for the search is because the child, the most important person in the relationship, and their need to know is as great *if not greater* than their birth mother's need to protect her secret.

Some APs spoke of their terror at the prospect of instigating an international birth-family search on behalf of their child and the uncertain nature of what could potentially emerge about their child's birth family. Many APs have expressed doubt about whether searching would be of benefit to the child and might even confuse them by expecting them to take in that they had another father and mother. The doubts expressed by APs are valid and understandable in the context of role handicap as it applies to adoptive parenthood – how am I to deal with another set of parents in this relationship? Notwithstanding the risks of instigating a search and having to deal with what might emerge, I faced into the unknown with the overwhelming feeling that this was ultimately the *right* thing for Kev and Tatiana.

The Collective Unconscious

Eminent Swiss psychologist Carl G. Jung (1981) writes of what he describes as the 'collective unconscious' and how a country's history can have a profound effect on the mindset of its natives. In a Catholic country where sex outside of marriage and single motherhood was regarded with stern disapproval, adoption is linked with the uncompromising attitudes of our past. Ruth Kelly writes of:

> The severe and judgemental attitudes towards women who became pregnant outside marriage or towards women who were caring for their illegitimate child permeated the ethos of many state and church agencies. Church and State were wedded in their conceptualisation of unmarried motherhood as problematic (2005, p. 3).

Mike Milotte (2012) outlines a number of adoption cases where blatant negligence and illegal practice meant that many babies were adopted in large numbers and went to America and as a result, many adopted people are unaware of their adoption, and those who are aware are unable to trace their birth history due to the falsification of essential records. In Ireland, thousands of adult adoptees are still searching for legally withheld birth information. The passing in 2015 of the Adoption Information and Tracing Bill has increased chances for Irish adoptees in obtaining birth information.

For Irish people born before the eighties and the 'fall' of the Church, who were reared under the heavy influence of Catholicism, the concept of adoption has a close association with the Church's dark past.

The idea, then, of an Irish AP actually searching for her child's birth family is an alien one. In the case of IA, searching for a birth family in a foreign country presents a range of challenges, not least of which is the emotional pressure of facing uncertainty about the personal circumstances of the birth family. Dealing with a foreign language and what can often be a stormy political climate adds a further layer of challenges for APs and adoptees.

As well as the influence of our Irish collective unconscious, APs are traditionally seen to benefit from the secrecy and silence around adoption in that professional advice has in the past advocated that to ensure the formation of a close bond, contact with the birth family should be avoided until the child reaches adulthood. It is not surprising, then, that Irish people are reluctant to delve into the adopted child's birth stories. Our collective unconscious lends itself toward secrecy in adoption.

Reactions

The Reaction of the Extended Family to the Search
'There are still those in our society who feel that searching adoptees are ungrateful and uncaring about their adoptive parents' feelings.' Nancy Newton Verrier, *The Primal Wound* (1993, p. 154).

In Joanne Trollope's 2004 novel, *Brother and Sister*, when the adopted daughter announces she is going to search for her birth mother, neither her adoptive mother nor her adoptive grandmother is impressed. The novel outlines the discomfort felt by the adoptive family, particularly the adoptive grandmother, who sees her position as being assailed by her granddaughter's decision to search. She ponders her status as a grandmother should another grandmother materialise as a result of the search.

An AP deciding to carry out a search is acting as a trustee for her child and seeking out precious information on her child's behalf. The AP is performing a task that may be best to keep confidential, and to be cherished within the confines of the parent-child adoptive relationship. All families are different, and the extent to which the AP decides to share the decision and/or outcome of the search depends on the dynamics within the family unit. However, while the search is being undertaken, it may be best to keep it under wraps, just between the child and APs.

Keeping secrets from members of the extended adoptive family might prove difficult. It is this aspect of searching that often prevents APs from searching for their child's birth family. It is pressure enough to engage in the unknown area of searching but having to worry about how members of the extended family might react adds a further layer of unease. Concern about the reactions of the extended family to a birth family search may deter the AP from carrying out the search in the first place. The extended adoptive family's anticipated reaction to a search is likely to impact on the decision to search, irrespective of whether it is the adopted parent or the adoptee initiating the search.

The Reaction of the Adult Adoptees to the AP's Search

Adult adoptees are puzzled when I mention to them how APs can search for their child's birth family. One adult adoptee was adamant that *only* the adoptee should search for birth information; it is not the AP's business, and searching should be left to the discretion of the adopted person. Another adult adoptee, while initially puzzled by my story of searching for my children's birth family, did agree that searching while the child is young and keeping information in trust for them until they are older is a helpful action.

A collection of over fifty adopted adult's writing, *Chosen: Living with Adoption*, was launched in Dublin in 2012. A number of the contributors were present at the launch and spoke about their experiences of adoption. One contributor, Catherine, talked of growing up not knowing her birth history, which she said her APs had kept from her in an attempt to shield her from pain. She said that: 'Our adoptive parents do not own our history, it belongs to us and should not be kept from us, no matter how bad the news.'

Reactions of Adult Adoptees to Search and Reunion

Searching for a birth connection is a common theme in the writings of adopted people. Reaction has been varied, but the thrust is the same: it is a blood trail. Here are some of the comments of adult adoptees:

'You cannot disown what is yours. There is always the return. And the wound will take you there. It is a blood-trail.' Jeanette Winterson (2011, p. 222).

'The loss of my birth parents, time in an orphanage and exile to a foreign country acted as a series of injuries that left me emotionally devastated. My life became a search, a quest to heal the suffering that stemmed from those early events.' Peter F. Dodds (1997, p. 1).

'The unseen bond originating in the womb at the time of conception, a link that forever connects mother and child, doesn't exist between adopted children and adopted mothers (p. 68). Mother is our first love affair. Her arms. Her eyes. Her breast. Her body. I guess I've been looking for us both all my life.' Peter F. Dodds (1997, p. 160).

'If you know you are adopted, […] you know that this first mum relinquished you and gave the right to love you to someone else. You know that she might have done this to offer you a chance at a better life, but it doesn't make you *feel* any better.' Clare Cashin (p. 15).

'Connection with our past, with our heritage. This is our *most* basic need as adults.' Sherrie Eldridge (2015, p. 175).

'I wanted to get to know my birth mother – whatever it took.' Aoife Curran (2013, p. 33).

Post-Reunion Perspectives

Ruth A. Moran, counsellor and adoptee, has written of the different stages of emotion in the wake of reunion with a birth mother, drawn from her own personal experience. Ruth Moran (1994) describes four stages: Paralysis, Eruption, Loss and Grief, and Empowerment.

Stage 1: Paralysis

There is an initial reaction of utter amazement and shock as the adoptee looks into the face of the person who gave them life. Ruth says that paralysis may arise from the simultaneous experience of so many emotions – the mind and soul are on overload. Physically, an overwhelming lethargy may set in, making routine tasks impossible.

Stage 2: Eruption

Ruth describes how emotions will wash over the adoptee like the 'after-shock of an earthquake'. During this stage the adoptee will have time to absorb the realities of their origins. It is the time when the fantasies about the biological mother and the circumstances surrounding the adoption must be laid aside. Although the truth may set one free, it is not always easy to face.

Stage 3: Loss and Grief

The realisation of loss of bonding in having been relinquished by the birth parents can be devastating for the adoptee. At this stage, Ruth states that the adoptee realises that the primary bonding cannot be recaptured. It will take time to move beyond this stage of loss and grief.

Stage 4: Empowerment

With acceptance comes a sense of self-empowerment. During empowerment, the adoptee moves beyond acceptance to the growth of a new self-knowledge and self-awareness.

Adoptee Stories about Search and Reunion

In TV3's highly successful documentary series, *Adoption Stories,* Sharon Lawless brings to the screen, in a sensitive and compelling way, stories from all sides of the adoption triad. Adoptees, birth mothers and APs share their stories of heartbreak and joy, of disappointment and fulfilment. Many stories are of long, unsuccessful searches, of further rejection by the birth family, of crashing disappointment by prospective APs, of utter heartbreak by birth mothers searching for lost children and of the utter ecstasy of reunion. Often while I watch a contributor speak of their longing to find their birth family, particularly their birth mother, determination thumps like a drum in my chest. Observing the travails of the adoptee as they struggle to find a birth relative is, for an AP, an emotionally charged experience. It makes me think of my own children and I pledge to do the best I can for them.

Adoptees have shared their experiences of search and reunion. Reading these writings is a valuable exercise for the AP. In her poignant memoir of search and reunion, Claire Cashin outlines how she reacted to reuniting with her birth parents, describes the complex mix of feelings upon seeing them for the first time and the tumultuous emotions that swept over her in the aftermath of the meeting. When the initial shock receded and explanations were offered as to why she was placed for adoption, Cashin describes her anger and resentment. She pondered why they couldn't have kept her, especially as they got married and started a new family within a year of giving her up. While she kept contact with them by letter after the reunion, she described the letters as

> … increasingly frustrated and less able to describe the spectrum of feelings we were both experiencing. Each time either Mai [the birth mother] or myself stated something in a letter to the other, we seemed to misunderstand what was meant, and anger and confusion began to grow. I think the depth of our feelings smothered us and our ability to talk to one another (2006, pp. 97–98).

Cashin also describes the empowerment she felt once she accepted the trauma of her adoption as part of her life. She concludes her wonderful memoir as follows: 'Second chances like this don't come around often, and I'll be damned if I'm going to make the same mistakes twice. I am truly blessed' (2006, p. 222).

Not all adoption reunions are successful, and in addition, many adoptees reflect on what might have been had they remained with their birth family and expressed gratitude for how their lives turned out. Jeanette Winterson, who described the adoption search as a 'blood trail', outlines her mixed and at times non-existent feelings at the outcome of reunion with her birth family.

> I know that Ann [birth mother] and Linda [birth aunt] want to include me in their family, that is their generosity. I don't want to be included: that is not my hard-heartedness. I am so glad to know that Ann survived and I like thinking of her surrounded by the others. But I don't want to be there. That's not what's important to me. And I don't feel a biological connection. I don't feel, 'Wow, here's my mother' (2011, p. 229).

Winterson also wrote at length about her difficult relationship with her adoptive mother, and expressed discomfort at her birth mother speaking ill of her adoptive mother:

> I hate Ann criticising Mrs Winterson. She was a monster but she was my monster [. . .] I would rather be this me – the me that I have become – than me I might have become without books, without education, and without all the things that happened to me along the way, including Mrs Winterson. I think I am lucky (2011, pp. 228–229).

The Search – A Personal Experience

For me, the search stretched over a number of years, beginning in 2006 when my first request was emailed to international birth family searchers Anna and Ruslan (See Useful Services). It continued for eight years until 2014 when, finally, a two-way connection was made. This is a chronological outline of how it all unfolded, beginning with the task of preparing a detailed information email for Ruslan before he made his journey to Russia and Kazakhstan. Searching for my children's birth family was not just about the administrative tasks of monitoring emails and digging into my savings for a searcher's travel costs. Searching and finding my children's birth families summoned the deepest and most conflicting emotions: sadness, anxiety and pure joy.

The Search in Two Parts

The search for Kev and Tatiana's birth families happened in two parts. Initially, Ruslan, a Ukraine-based international searcher and translator, travelled to both countries to find the birth families with the help of the information I had received at the time of their adoption. The second contact, which was made via social media, happened as a result of the search.

Armed with the information gleaned by Ruslan, it was then possible to search online and make contact with the birth families by email and Kontakte messenger (the Russian version of Facebook). It might have been possible to establish contact with the birth families without Ruslan's visits. However, sending the first social media messages to the birth families was made easier because of Ruslan's initial visit as there was a reference point – we introduced ourselves by mentioning his visit. It was also reassuring to know that Ruslan had spoken to both birth mothers, had confirmed their veracity, received photos, been welcomed with open-hearted joy and verified both birth mothers' knowledge of the children.

Searching

Searching for my children's birth information was emotionally demanding, expensive and time-consuming. It involved constructing a detailed portfolio for Ruslan to help him search, including photos and biographies of our children's progress to date. There were long-distance phone calls to the search co-ordinator, Anna; constant checking for replies to e-mails; and above all, a need for oodles of patience as long waiting periods elapsed.

Anna asked us to prepare a list of questions which she promised Ruslan would put to the birth mothers if he located them. If the AP has the name, address or date of birth of the birth mother, then a search is possible. If the AP has a name and little else, the searcher will naturally have to do more detection work, such as calling to the area of the child's orphanage/children's house and asking questions about the birth mother to try to ascertain her whereabouts. Depending on the searcher's attitude, making enquiries on a door-to-door basis about a woman who gave birth years ago will not, understandably, be something they wish to engage in. The searcher may feel that they are being unethical toward someone who may have been in a desperate state of penury or shame and posing questions about her could attract unwanted attention that may impact negatively on her. Such is the delicacy and complexity of the search operation.

The process can take several months from the time the AP initially contacts the searcher. The searcher will conduct a number of searches simultaneously for several families – searching is a commercial enterprise, after all. They will schedule their journey to the country when a number of requests to search have been received from APs.

Searching is their livelihood and a trip to a country as vast as Kazakhstan, for example, must have an economic return in order to make the trip viable. Therefore, the searcher will not travel to Kazakhstan unless they are searching for more than one family. When I contacted Ruslan (through Anna) with my request for a search, he had just returned from a search in Kazakhstan, and I then had to wait for nearly a year before he was due to travel again. In the context of wondering and uncertainty, it seemed like an eternity. In many ways, searching resembled the initial adoption process itself, so high was the emotional pressure and uncertainty due to the 'stop start' nature of it all.

What Was I Letting Myself In For?

I can understand why the APs I've spoken to about searching for a child's birth history expressed fear and reluctance at such a prospect. It's easier to pretend something isn't there than to look at it in the face and take the impact. The freezing fear I felt as I filled out the online form for Ruslan and Anna had me asking: *What am I letting myself in for?*

At the time of doing the initial search, both my children were getting on well. At ages eight and six, we had the usual day-to-day mundanity mixed with rollercoaster moments, as is the wont of parenthood. How could I introduce a subject so life-changing and significant without risking a reaction so extreme that I would rue the day I ever searched?

What if the news was damning and awful, that both birth families consisted of individuals to be avoided at all costs? Would it not be better, as the old saying goes, to 'leave well alone' or 'let sleeping dogs lie'? Should I just leave all this until they were both adults and able to deal with it independently rather than me having to endure it all now? During the schlep of getting the portfolio of information together for Ruslan, I continually asked myself why I was doing this at a time when there were so many other pressing things to get done. One evening I spent far too long typing Tatiana's information into an email for the searcher while Tatiana was waiting outside in the car for me to bring her to a football match. As I started the car, unable to explain why I got delayed as I wasn't going to reveal anything to her until the search was completed, there was a feeling of having switched back to reality after inhabiting the alternate universe of my daughter's birth family.

However, no matter what, the overwhelming conviction that I was doing the right thing drove me resolutely forward. I pressed the 'send' button on the last email, confirming intention to accept the searcher's terms and conditions (financial costs mostly), took a deep breath and settled in for a long wait.

It is best not to tell your child anything about the decision to search until you have definite, tangible news. This can be easy enough if your child is young, but once they hit the teen years, trying to furtively send and receive emails can become more difficult. As the custodian of your child and their birth information, and the person most impacted by their undulating emotions, the enormity of the task cannot be underestimated: searching for birth information, processing the information once it arrives and then communicating the information appropriately to your child is a huge task.

Reading the Searcher's Report

From the moment the searcher's emails appeared in the inbox, confirming that the birth mothers of both children had been found and the search was successful, that is, the birth family accepted a visit from the searcher, my heart was pounding and my brain on high alert. When undertaking to request the search, I had to accept the possibility that the searcher (a) might not find anyone or (b) find someone but be turned away and a meeting refused. To discover that this was not the case was extremely good news. It took over a week for the searcher to complete his report and soon it arrived with photographs. Receiving, reading and digesting the reports from both Russia and Kazakhstan was an incomparable experience. The most incredible moment was when I looked for the first time into a face as familiar as my own but totally unfamiliar at the same time. These strangers were familiar enough to share the facial features of my children but were otherwise completely unknown to both my children and me. Oh, the depth of emotions when I first looked into the faces of those genetically linked to the children I've known and loved since infanthood! Joy, fear, excitement, sorrow, relief, grief – all bundled together and thumped in my chest. I realised that if it felt so emotionally fraught for me, how would it be for my children?

The report arrived shortly after. I read about the talents of my children's birth families, their occupations, leisure pursuits and general achievements – this moment has frozen in my mind since. To say my heart was pounding in my ears is an understatement. Bit by bit the pieces of information sank in and my children's picture became complete. Discovering your child's birth heritage is like cataracts falling from your eyes, the images you might have had, if any, of where your child came from, become actual entities, fully formed in your mind's eye.

Reading their stories and seeing photos of their families allowed me to align myself to their tribe, to be connected to a part of them in a way I never expected. If seeing the birth family is integral to the adopted person's formation of identity, then I, as the person closest to them, also gained a stronger sense of closeness from making a connection with my children's birth family. This search for my children's birth family was as important for me, their AP, as it was for them.

The most I will say about what is a very private aspect of my children's life is that both have sprawling dynasties in their native countries. It is difficult to write this without feeling deep sadness. Once again, I am reminded that shame, societal pressure and economic deprivation are major drivers in the relinquishment and abandonment that is at the heart of adoption. As I read each report, I was hollow with sadness. It was hard not to empathise with the situations of both birth mothers and the desperation that led to the relinquishment of their beautiful children. The more I read, the more determined I became. Searching for my children's birth information made me even more resolute that connection had to happen, no matter how difficult, complicated or expensive it would be.

Telling My Children

'Many adoptees feel closer to their adoptive parents after reunion.' Betty Lifton, *Lost and Found* (1988, p. 180).

After the arrival of Ruslan's information, the words of a song from my childhood, by a band called the O'Jays, was on auto repeat in my head: 'Now that we've found love, what are we going to do with it?' Now that I have all this information, what in heck am I going to do with it? Another voice was there too. One that said 'Ok, Mari, so noble are you to have done this search. But now that you know all of this, you have to tell them. Was it not easier before, not knowing and having nothing to tell because you didn't know anything?'

From the adoption support team in Barnardos and the reading I did on the subject, I gleaned that the best thing to do was to give the information in age-appropriate stages – little bits at a time. As mentioned, Kev was eight and Tatiana was six. In Tatiana's case, on the advice of another AP, I slipped the newly received birth family photos into her life book. Apart from widening her eyes when she first saw the photo of her birth mother, she turned the page to the next photo, a familiar one already in her life book, and didn't make any initial comment. Questions followed later, but in the immediate aftermath of a successful (first) search, in Tatiana's case, the photos did all the 'telling'. At age six, Tatiana was too young to burden with the details of Ruslan's endeavours. Approximately three years later the questions came, but at that stage the presence of her birth family, through Ruslan's precious photos, was well established for her.

After Ruslan's search, Kev needed a more nuanced approach because of his age and because I didn't have any photos from the search to help me. I had to pick a time to tell him. When was a good time to do that in the busy vortex of life, driving here and there, juggling school and playtime? I didn't fancy telling him at bedtime as I reckoned trying to sleep after such tumultuous news might be tricky – for everyone. I seized a quiet moment in the swimming pool when Tatiana was having her lessons and Kev and I were splashing away together playing with a ball. I hugged him and plunged straight in (excuse the pun!), telling him we had employed a private detective who had found his birth mother, Inna. I told him that the detective had spoken with her and she had sent her love to Kev. I stared at his beautiful face as he took in the news, a grimace of anxiety, which was permanently on his forehead, miraculously, at that precise moment of telling him his birth mother had been found, smoothed out. At eight years of age, he couldn't fully grasp the enormity of what I was communicating to him, but he was close enough.

Familiar Faces of Intimate Strangers

The second part of the search for the birth families took place a few years later, when Kev was fourteen years old. We had been unable to establish ongoing contact with Kev's birth family since Ruslan's visit in 2006. Thanks to Phil's knowledge of the Russian language, he was able to type some of Kev's birth family details into Kontakte, such as their Russian surnames and dates of birth, information we got when we adopted Kev and also through Ruslan's 2006 search. The result took my breath away.

Words cannot describe how it felt to stare at an identical face, unmistakeably related by blood to my son, whom I had held in my arms since he was eight months old. When mulling over the extraordinary discovery of his birth family on social media, the immediate worry was how would Kev react to it. It was difficult not to be suffused with anxiety. It was one thing to convey a second-hand account from Ruslan of a meeting with a birth relative thousands of miles away, but a whole other thing to point out that a birth relative was as large as life and accessible on social media, regularly updating and posting photos.

However, my main thought was how could I not share this wonderful news with Kev? How could I live day after day with my child and not tell him that a close birth family member is alive and well and is the living image of him? I was also aware that many adopted people search for most of their lives and struggle to find a birth family member. Today, with the click of a button, I had unearthed priceless information. How could I not share it with him?

Birth Family on Social Media

After much mulling over how to tell Kev of the array of birth family photos on Kontakte, I simply asked him outright if he wanted to put their names in the search facility. If it was he who found them, it might be easier for him to process, rather than me announcing: 'Here, look who I found on Kontakte.' It took a few suggestions before he agreed to sit down in front of the family desktop and type in the birth names. He did not react much, initially, to the sight of so many recognisable faces posing happily for the camera, his birth brother in particular, who is the spitting image of him. Instead, he just reached for his Xbox controller and went back to his game. Suggestions that we send a direct message via Kontakte were met with a firm 'No'. I got the photos printed off for him and he kept them in his bedroom drawer. Every now and again I logged in to Kontakte, stalker-like, to look at his birth family.

Nearly two years elapsed after the first technological sighting of Kev's birth family before Kev requested that we make contact. His request to make contact was as a result of Tatiana's contact with her birth family. Upon hearing that Tatiana had made a connection, Kev decided the time was right and requested us to make contact on his behalf. Where there is more than one child in an adoptive family, there will be a dynamic around search and reunion – siblings will talk amongst themselves and compare notes on who is doing what with his or her birth family. I had not anticipated the influence of Tatiana making contact with her birth family might have on Kev. The searches were in two different countries, but the personal interaction between Kev and Tatiana had an impact on the sequence of events as they unfolded. Kev's decided to make contact by social media with his birth family; it was just before his Junior Certificate (State Examinations) and he was nearly sixteen.

He requested that we send a message to his birth sister, and as he was caught up in exam pressure, we decided it was sensible to wait until after he had completed his exams. Phil sent a message in Russian in which we introduced ourselves and referred to Ruslan's previous meeting in 2006 with Kev's birth mother. We felt such joy when almost immediately a message came back from his birth sister, filled with happiness and gratitude and dotted with emojis of love hearts and smiley faces. The email relationship was intense for about six or seven months. During that time, Kev described hearing from his birth sister as a 'weight being lifted from my shoulders'. Nearly three years later, contact is sporadic but still alive. Most important of all, the door is open for setting up a reunion whenever Kev is ready for such an event.

A Second Search in Kazakhstan

While we had located photos of Kev's birth family on Kontakte, finding Tatiana's birth family in Kazakhstan on social media proved more complicated. Even though the first 2007 search had yielded photos and family information, nearly six years had elapsed, and no further contact had been made. Tatiana had been asking about them and had spoken of feeling sad and in a low mood when she thought about her birth family.

In 2013, when Tatiana was twelve, I emailed Anna again and requested a second visit to Kazakhstan. My goal this time was to obtain an email address or Kontakte profile to maintain contact. While the initial search in 2007 was valuable, it represented a point-in-time contact only, whereas setting up ongoing contact was more important and essential in order to work toward reunion. When the report from the second search arrived, it included a link to Tatiana's birth sister's Kontakte profile as well as mobile phone numbers for all the birth family. The second search also yielded dozens of photos of Tatiana's birth siblings and birth mother, updates on family progress to date and miraculously, a DVD of the birth family speaking directly to Tatiana. This contact was what spurred Kev to connect with his birth family, as already outlined above.

Reunion by Social Media, Phone and Skype

Social Media

'Communication by social media, responsibly monitored, allows an emotional connection without the pressure of physical proximity and in the case of the complexity of adoption reunion, it can prove effective in building a gradual relationship.' Eileen Fursland, Facing up to Facebook Workshop, 2014.

There's some irony in my declaration that social media has afforded my children and me immeasurable joy and reassurance, given my ongoing and often expressed concerns about the negative impact of screen technology. Perhaps my experience of reunion by social media is an example of the diversity of technology – proof of the mixture of good and bad inherent in this modern miracle.

Phone

After Ruslan's second visit (2013) to Tatiana's birth family in Kazakhstan, there was still the question of maintaining ongoing communication. Despite having received a link to Kontakte through Ruslan's visit, we were unable to access Tatiana's birth sister's social media page. Phone numbers had been given by the birth family, but not feeling confident enough to hold a conversation of such high emotional velocity in the Russian language, despite Phil's progress with the language, we located a Kildare-based Russian translator, Olga Farrell.

The next step on the journey would not have been possible without the help of Olga, our wonderful Russian interpreter, who suggested she would call Tatiana's birth mother. On the day that Olga called me and said she had managed to speak with Marina, I felt nervous excitement well up. Could it be this easy, could establishing contact with Kazakhstan be as simple as a phone call? Olga then suggested a conference phone call between Tatiana and her birth family.

And so, on a sunny July afternoon in the Kildare countryside, on the sofa in Olga's beautiful sitting room, I awaited, with Tatiana, the response to Olga's attempts to get connected to Kazakhstan, thousands of miles away. As the phone dialled out over and over, I held my breath in fear of us having to leave Olga's house without having connected, having to deal with the blow of the family not being in the house to answer Olga's phone call as they had promised. The phone answered and what followed from the point of view of an adoptive mother could only be described as mind-blowing.

Olga spoke in gunfire-sounding Russian into the telephone speaker she had set up on the coffee table. A high-pitched voice responded, fast and excited. This was Tatiana's birth mother, Marina. Olga said, turning to Tatiana: 'They are all there. Marina is there, Anastasia is there and Zahar is there.' There were many 'slushitas', which I afterwards discovered meant 'listen', and many 'harashos', which means 'good'. Olga asked in a friendly, relaxed tone about the weather and holidays and the children being off school. When Marina answered, Olga would translate to English. Marina spoke to Tanya directly: 'Priviet, Tatiana', which meant 'Hi, Tatiana'.

The thrust of the conversation reminded me of relatives being united live on air by a presenter. The striking aspect of such emotion-laden conversations is the banality. Only single words are exchanged, and small talk is made. Significant conversation is not emotionally possible. Tatiana had zillions of questions to ask; Marina had zillions of memories flooding through her. It was obvious her voice was soaked and breaking with emotion. The safest route of sticking with small talk was taken – the weather and holiday plans.

While this landmark event was ongoing, I was happy to sit quietly on Olga's comfy sofa and watch Tatiana absorbing the miracle of speaking through an interpreter to her birth family. My role as the adoptive mother was to be there for Tatiana, to help her ease back into her life carrying the pain of loss, a loss that was further highlighted by making contact with the blood family she had been torn away from. It was both joyful and difficult to watch my lovely daughter hold back tears of joy and sorrow as she squeezed out a few words. Her most radiant smile was when her birth brother, Zahar, in his deep, manly voice, enunciated loudly across the speaker 'Priviet, Tatiana'.

As we drove away that day in the July sunshine, stopping in Roberstown to buy ice cream and eating it perched on a wall in the village, it did feel as if something very significant had happened, as if the Rubicon had been crossed, as if anything was now possible. A few days later, as I have done in the wake of any significant birth family events, I brought Tatiana for a visit to the Barnardos post adoption service, where she recounted her tumultuous experience to a captive and empathic listener.

Skype

Our next (social media) reunion was fifteen months later, in October 2015, when Tatiana spoke by Skype with her birth sister, who was by then attending the State University in Semey, Kazakhstan. Once again, I was the adoptive mother on the side-line as Tatiana, with the help of Olga, spoke for an hour and a half with her birth sister and discovered similar tastes in reading and movies, particularly the *Harry Potter* series, where they shared the same favourite character, Ron Weasley, and the same favourite Hogwarts house, Gryffindor. Both girls emitted similar giggles which littered their animated conversation. At one point, after lurking in the shadows, I came forward to say 'Strasvacha' ('Hello' in Russian) into the screen where Anastasia's bright, smiling face was. My voice emerged weirdly high-pitched, reflecting my mixed emotions: excitement, uncertainty, shyness, self-consciousness and a touch of peevishness at my inability to offer any relevant input. The room was overpoweringly warm, or at least it seemed to be, and the conversation dragged on, but I felt I had relinquished authority over my daughter. Role handicap overcame me. How does an adoptive mother act when her daughter re-connects by Skype with her long-lost birth sister?

Afterwards, I know that Tatiana struggled with conflicting emotions as a result of coming into close contact, albeit by technology, with her sister from whom she had been separated since she was born. At fourteen years of age, having to continue on with her life as if nothing happened, as if everything was the same, when it clearly wasn't, proved difficult. As parents we did note how this impacted on her in the months following the Skype reunion. Tatiana spoke of the pain of being tantalisingly close to someone she wanted to get to know and be physically near to but not being able to do so. Her experience of speaking with other adoptees offered an opportunity to exchange similar experiences of tracing and she has acknowledged how far she has engaged with her birth family, often a source of wonder to other adoptees.

However, Tatiana speaks of the ongoing pain of separation which remains, despite the social media reunion. Her words capture the essence of how bittersweet a reunion is for an adoptee from another country, thousands of miles away from their country of birth. 'It's like looking at a thickly layered, delicious chocolate cake and being told you can only have a tiny slice, and as you long for more, the cake sits untouched in front of you, tempting you.' This metaphor sums up the bittersweet miracle of being able to see and hear your birth family despite the barrier of distance, and then having to switch off the device and accept that they are, for now, physically out of bounds.

Some reservations arose for me, such as the sense of not being part of the reunion or of being excluded from their indelible bond, but as I sat watching my daughter reconnect with her birth family, my main emotions were joy and an assurance that I had done the right thing. Too often I have learned of reunions where years have passed and vital people have died or a lack of information has destroyed all chances of reunion. The privilege of being part of Tatiana's reunion by technology suffused me with so much joy.

Does Connecting with the Birth Family Help?

'Finding their birth parents – either discovering more information about them or actually making direct contact – can be an enormous relief for a teenager.' Brodzinsky et al., (1993, p. 113).

The answer to this question depends on the circumstances – birth history, the disposition and accessibility of the birth family, and the adoptive family's emotional ability to deal with the complexities of interaction. The views expressed by adoptees in relation to the separation from their birth families certainly imply that having some sort of contact in their lives is beneficial. However, the whole aspect of communicating the information as well as monitoring and moderating contact to ensure that the child's emotional well-being is protected is a minefield for APs and an additional parenting pressure.

On one hand, you want more than anything to do what is best for your child, and on the other, you can clearly see the pitfalls from telling too much at too young an age or opening the door so wide that your child naturally wants to march through, irrespective of the consequences. Getting the balance right between keeping the reality of the birth family in your child's mind, communicating available information in an age-appropriate way and keeping focussed on the here and now – the life they are leading – these are the challenges faced by APs who open or semi-open an IA.

I have to stress the importance of professional support to accompany the AP and child along the journey of search and reunion. At each significant point in Tatiana's journey, I was fortunate enough to have the support of the Post Adoption Service of Barnados at various milestones. Having a contact outside the circle of the family unit, a compassionate, professional listener whom Tatiana could recount her story to was an essential aspect of introducing Tatiana to her birth family at such a relatively young age. The recounting of her joy, worry, sadness, hopes and dreams allowed her to process the tumultuousness that is birth family reunion.

Conclusion

Modern adoption is moving on. Attitudes have become more enlightened. With the advent of Facebook and air travel and (mostly) stable international political regimes, the re-uniting with a birth family from abroad is not the insurmountable barrier it once was. Open-mindedness is breaking down the barrier of stigma. APs in the past may not have discussed adoption with their children, but modern APs foster an open approach. The days of whispering and shushing are slowly melting away in favour of talk and discussion. There's a better chance now that a teenager adopted internationally will have ample information on their birth parents, can keep in contact with them, and has a strong chance of reuniting with them in the future. It is my dream to meet both birth mothers one day and be able to thank them in person. My dream also involves a conversation where we agree that rearing the children to the current point has been a collaborative effort – with them giving birth and me doing the rest. Adopted people can love their APs and still want to search. This is something APs and adoptees both need to understand. The two things are not either/or. Both can happen simultaneously.

Chapter Eight

PARENTHOOD FOR THE ADOPTED PERSON

'I was delighted to become a mother. For the first time, I saw
myself reflected back in my son's face; it was a powerful
and moving experience. For the first time, I had a living
connection to my genetic self.'

Bridget Betts, *Chosen*

Becoming a parent is a milestone in any life. For the adopted person,
it has particular implications. As previously touched on, Erik Erikson,
the Danish-born psychoanalyst, developed a model of the psychosocial
tasks that people confront as they move from infancy to old age. His
young adulthood stage, which he summarises as intimacy versus isolation, has specific challenges for the adopted person, including:

- the exploration of adoption as it relates to the growth of self and
  the development of intimacy;
- the consideration of a search for birth history and;
- the facing of unknown genetic information in light of the birth of
  children.

In the following section, I will outline the words of adopted people as
they express their emotions in relation to this momentous event.

Becoming A Parent

(All citations in this section are attributed to Brodzinsky et al., 1993.)
Adopted people have spoken of the significance of becoming
parents. Being connected to someone in a genetic way often satisfies

a primal desire and assuages any yearning for their own birth information. An adopted adult described to me the significance of having given birth to five children and how she viewed her children as her genetic connection. This was enough for her, and she no longer felt the need to search for her birth family. However, in many cases, becoming a parent for the first time can arouse conflicting emotions.

When the new parent is an adoptee, the universal urge to 'undo parent's mistakes' means not just the mistakes of the APs but the birth parents also. Sometimes this urge is expressed quite literally. Beth, single and aged twenty-three, considered her choices when she got pregnant – having an abortion or placing the child up for adoption. The thought of relinquishing her child recalled her own sense of loss. Beth said she didn't want to repeat the choice made by her birth mother and she chose to have an abortion. Beth said: 'I'd rather abort my baby than have it go through what I experienced' (p. 133).

The birth of a child often brings the adoptee into contact with the first person to whom they are biologically connected. This can have a profound effect. The birth of a child may force an adoptee to confront for the first time the lack of blood link with the people who loved and raised them. After she became a mother, Lynn stunned herself by resenting the security her baby would have from living with her biological parents. She also began a search for her birth parents soon after her baby was born:

You can't imagine what it was like when my daughter was born. I realised she was part of me, flesh and blood. She carried my genes – both good and bad ones – and would begin to resemble part of me, both physically and behaviourally, as she started to grow. When I realised this, I was surprised by my sense of jealousy. All my life I had lived at a disadvantage. I never knew who my biological parents were, what they looked like, what they did, what skills and talents they possessed, what shortcomings they had, etc. The funny thing is that I never consciously focussed on these issues when I was growing up (p. 135).

Mark, who had never consciously grieved the loss of his biological parents until he was twenty-eight and his first child was born, said:

'I saw her come out, and the first thing I noticed was her big nose – a nose that looked like mine. Then it hit me like a sledgehammer. My daughter was the first blood relative I had ever met' (p. 134).

The birth of a baby may reawaken issues of genetic isolation that were a feature of the adoptee's adolescence and which they thought had been resolved when adulthood was reached. Maria said: 'I had terrible postnatal depression, worse than any of the moods I had gone through in adolescence. I think it was because I was grieving all over again for the fact that I didn't have what my baby had – a mother who wanted him and kept him' (p. 135).

Beatrice, who dreaded giving birth because of the potential of some previously unknown genetic defect suddenly emerging in her own children said 'I was afraid to start a family. How could I explain a child that didn't look like me? Consequently, I have never borne a child. I regret that' (p. 131).

Implications for the Next Generation

If anything makes a young person truly move into adulthood, it's becoming a parent. For the adoptee, parenthood raises issues that are different from the ones raised for new parents who were not adopted. Even while planning a pregnancy, and certainly as the due date approaches, an adoptee may think for the first time about the possibility of passing on genetic problems they know nothing about. The absence of a genetic history takes on a greater magnitude when it is cast in the context of the next generation. Once an adoptee has children, the void in their own past is no longer theirs alone – it becomes their children's legacy. Their children are now also touched by adoption and may be the ones who request to learn about the parent's birth history. Also, the adoptee's partner can express a wish to learn of birth information to help with any family medical issues.

A recent feature on *The Ryan Tubridy Show* on RTÉ Radio One illustrated the dilemma of the spouse of an adoptee. The woman, who wished to remain anonymous, wrote to the show describing her distress at the stance of her husband in relation to seeking out his own birth information. The couple's children were growing up and she wanted to tell them that their father was adopted and also have information to share about his blood relatives, who were also their blood relatives. She referred to feeling anxious due to the fact that husband was born in Ireland; it is such a small country so there is a possibility that their children might encounter genetic relatives living in Ireland, unaware of the blood connection. In her view, their children were being deprived of another set of potential relatives who could enrich their lives, but any mention of telling the children was immediately rejected by her husband, who emphasised the closeness of his bond with his APs and refused to even discuss the issue.

Responses from the public to the woman's letter were varied and portrayed the diversity of views where openness in adoption is concerned. The first tranche of responses urged the woman to leave her husband's private business alone, to get on with her life and not to 'build a cross for her back' by pushing into an area that could bring trouble on herself and her family. However, as the responses continued, they became more nuanced in ethos, demonstrating the complexities of adoption. Many listeners touched by adoption described their own sorrows around deception and concealment of birth information in adoption and the impact of such deception on their lives. One listener described the distress endured by her husband as a consequence of his older (non-adopted) sisters concealing birth information from him over the years, an action which culminated in his birth mother dying before he managed to finally unearth his birth information. Ryan read out my own contribution as the closing letter on the feature:

I am the adoptive mother of two teenagers aged fifteen and seventeen and have lived through the gamut of varied emotions that is the lot of those of us touched by adoption. My husband and I have always been open with our children. In order to equip myself with the tools to deal with whatever being an adoptive parent might throw at me, I have, at this stage, read my way through a lexicon of adoption writing. The same theme runs through each and every book – every adopted person wonders at some point about their birth history – what they do about it varies from person to person, but the wondering remains. Another constant theme in adoption writings is the importance of openness – when someone keeps information secret on something as primal as one's origin and the truth surfaces, as it invariably does, feelings of hurt and betrayal follow.

The letter writer's husband has the right to decide whether or not he wishes to search for his birth family. That is his right. However, in refusing to be open with his children about the absence of bloodlink with his (adoptive) parents and by extension their absence of bloodlink with their (adoptive) grandparents, he is keeping information about their origins from them.

As he is confident of his bond with his adoptive parents, there is no reason why he should be afraid to tell his children about being adopted.

However, the husband's dismissal of the importance of discussing his adoption may well be denial on his part, as well as fear of the very pertinent questions his children will very likely ask and the buried emotions that might arise for him when those answers have to be given – answers which he probably doesn't have.

The saying 'Let sleeping dogs lie' is often the guiding mantra of adopted people and adoptive parents. However, the saying 'Silence is the greatest lie' has been shown to be more fitting.

The writer of the letter could get adoption support if she wishes – professional help is out there, details of which I can provide if required.

I wish her the very best.

Conclusion

The whole issue of the adoption conversation is as relevant in the case of the next generation as it is between AP and child – the same tenets apply. It is likely that the openness experienced by the adoptee growing up will be mirrored in their attitude toward talking about their adoption and their feelings about it with their own child. If adoption was something that was treated as a secret, rarely spoken about, and with an aura of shame or stigma floating around it, as projected by the APs, then such an attitude is likely to be carried into the next generation.

Chapter Nine

EVERYTHING IS A MIRACLE

'I believe the pain inflicted by the initial separation can be healed by loving, understanding adoptive parents and that adopted children can thrive if their new family is carefully prepared for the upcoming challenges.'

Sunny Jo Johnsen, *Adoptionland*

'I am eternally grateful for two extraordinary gifts: my writing ability, such as it is, and most importantly, my experience of adoption. Given the choice, I would not change a thing.'

Vanessa Gebbie, *Chosen*

'Adoption experts are wrong, wrong, wrong. Separation and loss are neither innately powerful nor irreparable; they are universal and ultimately impotent.'

Sally Bacchetta, *What I Want My Adopted Child to Know*

As the title of this section suggests, this is where I reflect on the miracles associated with adoption and record the upbeat voices of adult adoptees as they share their insights. In this chapter, I mull over concepts such as plasticity and recasting and reflect on how obstacles (as we perceive them) thrown our way, take our lives in different directions to what we had planned. I cite some arguments made against the existence of loss in adoption as a lifelong wound.

There are many references to loss and hurt in *Becoming a Mother*. Ultimately, hope and optimism is everything; it is all we have. A. M. Homes, adoptee, opens her 2007 memoir, *The Mistress's Daughter* with words from

Albert Einstein: 'There are two ways to live your life, one as though nothing is a miracle, the other as if everything is a miracle.' Most of us might sit somewhere in between the two extremes of Einstein's theory of life, living as if some, but not all, of life events are a miracle. Believing everything is a miracle brings light and sweetness in abundance.

Plasticity

Plasticity is a concept, like Bowlby's attachment theory, that presents itself as music to the ears of the AP. Irrespective of what an individual has suffered early in life, the love of an attentive, caring family will go a long way toward healing previous hurts.

The brain stays 'plastic', or changeable, into adulthood. Previously, it was believed that whatever damage happened in childhood was untreatable unless addressed in childhood. However, the brain can adapt to favourable conditions. In her 2001 book, *Life Span Development,* occupational psychologist Leonie Sugarman writes:

> Plasticity is concerned with the potential for directional change within an individual – the extent to which a developmental path can be altered once it has began. Thus, improved diet and an emotionally, intellectually and socially enriching environment can ameliorate much thwarted development in a child whose life has been characterised by multiple deprivations (2001, p. 18).

In short, change is possible. New habits, behaviours and attitudes can be learned at almost any age – a concept that is relevant to any aspect of human behaviour or experience, not solely adoption outcomes.

This message, taken from Apollo Counselling Dundrum's inspirational website (www.apollocounsellingdundrum.com) sums up the core message of brain plasticity: 'Never be a prisoner of your past. It was just a lesson, not a life sentence.'

Recasting

Another concept that fits with the miraculous and empowering journey of adoption is the concept of 'recasting', where one must find the positive in whatever life throws at you. The image conjured is that of reshaping something that is not as we want it into something else, the recasting of it into a work of beauty.

Dr Patricia Collard writes:

When you respond to adversity (such as a chronic condition, the loss of physical abilities or the death of a loved one) wisely and mindfully, you don't just 'get on with it' or 'look on the bright side'. You give yourself permission to feel the gravity of your pain or loss, without censoring it and with an attitude of honouring what you truly feel and experience. After accepting the sorrow of what happened, you wisely and compassionately see whether you can turn the experience around and view what lies on the opposite side of the 'shadowland'. You search for opportunities or insights that may come in handy from now on. By applying mindfulness and acceptance, you can gain the strength to transform yourself purposefully, instead of becoming a slave to the sadness of loss and pain (2013, p. 287).

In the case of adoption, grief may be present, but it is individual, intensely private and entirely surmountable. Those who undergo adoption grief do not wish to carry their experience of adoption around like a ball and chain. Dr Perlitta Harris accurately describes it in her introduction to *Chosen: Living with Adoption*: 'We [adoptees] offer advice for accepting one's adoption and moving forward as complete humans, rather than living as a wounded person' (2012, p. 9).

Harris also notes that the contributors to *Chosen* wrote of the 'rich lived experience that comes with adoption' and how experience of adoption shapes 'who we are and how we see ourselves, and as such, adoption is a gift, a bitter-sweet gift, that adopted people should be proud of' (p. 11).

David Brodzinsky and others include voices of many adoptees in *Being Adopted: The Lifelong Search for Self*. One such voice is that of Bertha, a seventy-three-year-old woman who was adopted in infancy:

As I look back on my life, I realise that being adopted has had some effect on me. But it has been quite small compared to everything else. There have been sad times, confusing times, times of curiosity, and angry times. Most of all adoption has just been a fact of life – a kind of backdrop in my life. Always there but simply taken for granted (1993, p. 193).

Claire Cashin, in her memoir of adoption and reunion with her birth family, writes:

When trying to describe what I felt throughout the years, I am worried that it will read like some terrible saga, without hope, without an end. But it is a happy story. Any instance when we are lucky enough to rediscover ourselves and manage to become whole is an amazing gift [...] it's just [adoption] is a process we have to reason out, in our own time, like any challenge or loss that is faced in life. Nothing is insurmountable (2006, p. 48).

Once, when I commented to a friend who is not touched by adoption, that adopted people grieve for the family they could have had, she replied: 'They got another family instead, a family they would not have known had they not been adopted.'

The greatest example of recasting for me has been my own experience of adoptive parenthood. Focussing on the sad parts of adoption helped me achieve balance in my attitude toward my children's loss. It would be untrue for me to say that I have not wondered what it might be like to have a child in my life who resembled me, in whom I could see aspects, physical and behavioural, that were familiar. However, these were thoughts that flitted in and out of my head amidst the hurly burly of parenting. Any regret I have harboured from not having given birth has been assuaged by the joy, fulfilment, contentment and adventure of having Kev and Tatiana in my life.

You Are Different Because You Are You

The impact of the primal wound in adoption is often the subject of contention. Sally Bacchetta, adoptive mother, argues against the held view that adopted people suffer a profound, primal loss. In her book, *What I Want My Adopted Child To Know: An Adoptive Parent's Perspective,* she passionately and eloquently outlines the varied ways in which we all suffer loss and overcome it:

> Our first separation doesn't slice at the depths of who we are. In fact, it cuts us free to become who we might. It doesn't create psychic scar tissue for us to heal around: it allows us to realise the fullness of our psychic potential. Rather than surviving in spite of the cut, we exist because of it (2010, p.78).

Bacchetta challenges negativity toward adoption in the following way:

> If it's true that adoption sentences adoptees to an unwinnable marathon for identity and integration, for attachment and belonging, how can it be that most adopted teens are as deeply attached to their parents as non-adopted teens? Why do most of them say they feel positively about their identity? How can it be that for most adopted adolescents, adoption is something they accept as a fact of life? And why are so many people who were not adopted exhausting themselves in the same race for meaning? Why do so many who were not adopted experience a similar search for meaning and feelings of alienation and depression similar to what some adoptees report? (p. 39)

Bacchetta also writes: 'You are not different because you were adopted, you are different because you are you. You have the same opportunities as the rest of us to grow, mature and adapt' (p. 32).

Individuality and the Jungian image of the 'wounded child' is explored by John Bradshaw as he urges for adult exploration of grief and loss in childhood as a way of purging demons and reaching actualisation. The uniqueness of each person is a key aspect of Bradshaw's work with the 'wounded inner child'. Another key aspect of his work warns that to get bogged down in your wounded personal history is never to get beyond your wounds.

Bradshaw concludes with a quotation by James Joyce from *A Portrait of the Artist as A Young Man*: 'Welcome, O life! I go to encounter for the millionth time the reality of experience and to forge in the smithy of my soul the uncreated conscience of my race' (1992, p. 285).

Being with Adult Adopted People

As an AP, hearing adopted adults speak about their experiences, whether positive or negative, is always significant, thought-provoking and entirely uplifting. Over the years, I have had the honour of listening to many adopted adults tell their stories, and whether the stories are ones of anger toward their APs or birth family, the very fact that these articulate, fully living, fully actualised people are in front of me, reflecting on their lives, illustrates to me that they have got there. Mostly, I just love mingling with adopted adults, being offered a window into their lives and witnessing the finished person, whole and extraordinary. I gravitate toward, and feel connected to, the adopted person, grown and complete.

My most uplifting night was the Irish launch of *Chosen: Living with Adoption,* where a host of adopted adults, who were contributors to the book, spoke of their childhoods with their respective adoptive families and the impact of their birth history on their lives. Many spoke of disappointment and rejection, their stories varied and complex, as with any family. The most encouraging aspect was to see the successful lives of these people and how they have survived adoption, irrespective of the challenges. I think that what an AP wants most of all is to see their child reach adulthood as fulfilled as possible. And this is what I saw at the launch of *Chosen.* Yes, many of the attendees nursed bitterness about their adoptive families, the secrets in their past and their difficult birth history. But the gripes were justified and related to the normal sadness experienced by any family – parental break-ups, relationship difficulties and disappointments. The most memorable was a woman describing her search for her birth mother and the series of let-downs she suffered as a result of her birth mother not turning up to arranged meet-ups. The woman spoke eloquently and honestly, and her confident demeanour in the face of the adversities life had thrown at her was a joy to behold. Overcoming hurdles like these is one of the most important aspects of life.

PJ Gallagher, popular Irish comedian and radio presenter, has spoken in various media interviews and conferences (notably the 2014 International Adoption Annual Conference which I also attended) about his adoption. He has referenced the manner in which adoption is often negatively portrayed and has spoken about his own happiness and contentment with his adoptive family and with his adoption in general. During his presentation at the conference, PJ spoke of his belief that happy adoptees are more common than unhappy ones, and indeed may be the 'silent majority'.

PJ is a great advocate for adoption and as an AP it is beyond wonderful to witness the amazing person the adoptee has become. A common thread with PJ's story, as with other adoptee's stories, is the search for their birth family, a story he has generously shared on a number of radio and television shows. PJ spoke to Ciara Dwyer in July 2017 in the *Sunday Independent*'s *Life* magazine about his adoption; he illustrated the understanding and empathy his adoptive mother shows toward his birth family: 'I have two mothers, because I was adopted. Every Mother's Day, my mother reminds me to call my mother.'

In the article, PJ described his search for his birth family stemming from a need for medical history. He met his birth family in 2001. 'My (birth) parents married after they had me and went on to have other children. So I gained a whole new crew. When I first looked at my sister, it blew me away, because we looked so alike. Neither of us could talk. It was so unnerving.'

The bond between PJ and his adoptive mother has obviously not been impacted by his search for and reunion with his birth family: 'I'm very close to my [adoptive] ma. I call up to her or talk to her at least once every day. She always knows best and this can be very annoying. If I need advice or am worried about something, I always talk to her' Dwyer (2017).

The Family of Things

Sellotaped to my kitchen cabinet is Mary Oliver's 'Wild Geese', which speaks to me of belonging and self-forgiveness. She urges us to speak to each other with compassion: 'Tell me about your despair, yours. And I will tell you mine.' We are all part of the 'family of things' and we do not have to be perfect all the time. This poem could also have resonance for the adoptee, who might, at times, express feelings of not belonging in any single family or culture. Oliver, who is American and still living and writing, assures us that no matter how glum or lonely we are feeling, we are all part of the one family. If you are not familiar with Mary Oliver's 'Wild Geese', it is worth it to read the poem in full.

AFTERWORD

'Parenting takes us places emotionally that we may never have travelled before, truly one of the precious gifts our children give us.' Daniel Hughes and Jonathan Baylin.

Becoming a mother via adoptive parenting has taken me places biological parenting would never have – for that I am eternally grateful. Adopting a child from another country has bolstered my empathy toward other cultures. Learning about the intricacies of adoption gave me a deep understanding of loss and has led to a career in psychotherapy. Two decades on, uttering the words 'My children', even in casual conversation, has the power to give me a dart of pure happiness.

From the early attempts to scribble down a record of milestone events to the point where a sustained piece of work emerged, this book has been as much a journey as becoming a mother has. The recounting of my personal story and the revelation of my deepest feelings has been daunting. In the words of American poet Robert Lowell in his poem 'Epilogue' as he urges the recording of the truth: 'Yet, why not say what happened?' Without offering an authentic part of myself, reflections on adoptive parenthood emerge as no more than arid theory without substance or depth.

Recently, upon hitting the ripe young age of fifty-seven years old, I was asked by Tatiana if I felt as if my life had flown past and if I was sad about how quickly I had reached this big age. I was happy to reply that yes, my life had flown past, but that I was content to report few regrets about how my life had panned out. Afterwards, I reflected on her incisive question and was aware, not for the first time, that becoming a mother was far and ahead the most ground-breaking event in my life and becoming an adoptive mother a key part of the ground-breaking event of motherhood. The richness I have been gifted as a consequence of Kev and Tatiana's existence in my life is immeasurable, and I thank God every day for their loving and inspirational presence.

The most fitting way to conclude what I hope is a blended view of adoption supported by a consortium of voices is to issue a heartfelt 'Thank you' to two very special women. While striving to put together a piece of writing commensurate with the significance of their roles in my life, I happened upon a competition in a Sunday newspaper called 'The Letter I Wish I'd Sent'. Readers were asked to submit a letter to the newspaper addressed to someone to whom they wanted to communicate a profound message but hadn't for a variety of reasons. I will conclude by reprinting a letter signed 'Name and address with editor', published in the *Sunday Independent* on 25th June 2017. It was a letter that lifted my heart for two reasons. Firstly, it articulated precisely what I wanted to say and secondly (when I read the many laudatory comments online), it reassured me that many APs think about their child's birth mother just as much as I do. Heartfelt thanks to the letter writer for her eloquent and gracious articulation of gratitude. I wish her every happiness. Her adherence to the spirit of collaboration between adoptive mother and birth mother can only bring the best for her child.

To the birth mother of my child,

I think of you very often, your face like a photograph imprinted in my mind, sometimes when I look at my adored child, your son, our son, I see you in him and I wonder if you also laugh like he does, if you tense your mouth the way he does when he's excited, if you think of him often, if you cherish the time you spent with him, if you regret...

I picture you when you were pregnant, I try to imagine the moment when you gave birth to him, what did you feel when you held him?

I try to imagine the days you spent together when you took good care of him. I try to imagine the long and tortuous journey you both endured to his temporary home, knowing these would be the last moments you would spend with him, how did you say goodbye? How did you go on after that?

I try to imagine how his life would be with you, without me. There are no words to describe how I feel about you and the decision you made which changed my life forever. No words but so many feelings.

Like me, you are a mother, you know what it is to love unconditionally, to feel your child's pain in your own body, to feel danger before it even exists, to want the world and some more for your child, to sacrifice your own happiness for his. You took all of that to a different level the moment I became his mother. Your loss was my gain: your sorrow was the happiest moment of my life.

When I hold my adored son – your son, our son – I want to stop the time and thank you and the universe for this gift and privilege I certainly did nothing to deserve.

I know this won't fill the immense hold his absence left in your heart, I know it won't replace the irreplaceable: your son, your beautifully perfect son. But I want you to feel the love I pour on him every second of the day.

I hope somehow this letter gets to you, so you know that he is very much loved, and always will be.

The mother of your child.

References

Adoption Authority of Ireland (AAI) Annual Report (2016).

Ainsworth, M.D.S. (1970) 'Attachment, Exploration, and Separation: Illustrated by the Behaviour of One-Year-Olds in a Strange Situation' in *Child Development*, 41(1): 49–67.

Anonymous. (2017) 'The Letter I Wish I'd Sent' in *The Sunday Independent*. Dublin.

Amos, H. and Rankin, J. (2012) 'How Many Kids Are in Institutions? No Way to Know'. *The Moscow Times*, 29 March 2012. Available from: http://www.russialist.org/archives/russia-orphans-numbers-670.php

Bacchetta, S. (2010) *What I Want My Adopted Child to Know*. Bloomington: iUniverse.

Barry, H. and Murphy, E. (2014) *Flagging the Screenager: Guiding your Child Through Adolescence and Young Adulthood*. Dublin: Liberties Press.

Bowlby, J. (1969) *Attachment and Loss, Volume One*. New York: Basic Books.

Bradshaw, J. (1992) *Homecoming: Reclaiming and Healing your Inner Child*. New York: Bantam Books.

Brodzinsky, D.M., Schechter, M.D., and Marantz H. (1993) *Being Adopted: The Lifelong Search for Self*. New York: Anchor Books.

Carp, E.W. (1998) *Family Matters: Secrecy and Disclosure in the History of Adoption*. Massachusetts: Harvard University Press.

Carter, J. and Carter, M. (1989) *Sweet Grapes: How to Stop Being Infertile and Start Living Again*. Indianapolis: Perspectives Press.

Cashin, Claire. (2006) *Will You Be Here When I Get Home?* Dublin: Mercier Press.

Collard, P. (2013) *Mindfulness-Based Cognitive Therapy for Dummies*. Chichester: John Wiley and Sons.

Cronin, A. (2014) 'Poetry Column', *The Sunday Independent*. Dublin: 10 August 2014.

Curran, A. (2013) *Searching For Me: My Adoption Story*. Dublin: Emu Ink.

Dodds, P.F. (1997) *Outer Search, Inner Journey: An Orphan and Adoptee's Quest*. Washington: Aphrodite Publishing Company.

References

Dodds, P.F. (2015) 'The Parallels between International Adoption and Slavery' in *Sociology Between the Gaps: Forgotten and Neglected Topics* (1): 76–81.

Doka, K. (1989) *Disenfranchised Grief: Recognizing Hidden Sorrow*. US: Lexington Books.

Dusky, L. (1979) *Birthmark*. New York: M. Evans & Company, Inc.

Dwyer, C. (2017) 'Waking Hours' in *Sunday Independent, Life Magazine*. Dublin.

Eldridge, S. (1999) *Twenty Things Adopted Kids Wish Their Adoptive Parents Knew*. New York: Bantam Dell.

Eldridge, S. (2015) *Twenty Life-Transforming Choices Adoptees Need to Make*. London: Jessica Kingsley Publishers.

Erikson, E. (1950) *Childhood and Society*. New York: W.W. Norton & Company.

Ertman, M. (2015) *Love's Promises: How Formal and Informal Contracts Shape All Kinds of Families*. Boston: Beacon Press.

Edwards, J. and Dusky, L. The First Mother Forum. http://www.firstmotherforum.com/

Frym, G. (1989) 'Strange Fruit' in Chester, L. (ed.) *Cradle and All: Women Writers on Pregnancy and Birth*. Winchester: Faber and Faber.

Gallagher, M. (1999) 'From Russia with Love' in *Medicine Weekly*, (3): 26.

Gerhardt, S. (2004) *Why Love Matters*. London: Routledge.

Glasser, W. (1998) *Choice Theory: A New Psychology of Personal Freedom*. New York: Harper Collins.

Gobbel, R. (2016) 'Where There Is adoption, There Is Grief' in *Parenting, Adoption and Adoptive Parenting*. Available from: https://gobbelcounseling.wordpress.com/2016/07/15/where-there-is-adoption-there-is-grief/.

Harris, T. (1973) *I'm OK – You're OK*. New York: Avon.

Harris, P. (ed.) (2012) *Chosen: Living with Adoption*. London: British Association for Adoption and Fostering (BAAF).

Hoksbergen, R.A.C. (1997) *Child Adoption: A Guidebook for Adoptive Parents and Their Advisors*. London: Jessica Kingsley Publishers.

Holmes, J. (1993) *John Bowlby and Attachment Theory*. London: Routledge.

Homes, A.M. (2007) *The Mistress's Daughter*. London: Granta Publications.

Houghton, J. (2006) *A Forever Family*. London: Faber and Faber.

Howe, D. (2009) 'Nature, Nurture and Narratives' in Wrobel, G.N. and Neil, E. (eds.) *International Advances in Adoption Research for Practice*. Chichester: Wiley Blackwell.

References

Hughes, D.A. and Baylin, J. (2012) *Brain-Based Parenting: The Neuroscience of Caregiving for Healthy Attachment*. New York: W. W. Norton & Company.

International Adoption Association Ireland. (2014) 'Presentation to the Joint Committee on Health and Children on Adoption in Ireland and Related Matters', 26 June 2014.

Irwin Johnston, P. (1992) *Adopting After Infertility*. Indianapolis: Perspectives Press.

Jung, C.J. and Hull, R.F. (1981) *The Archetypes and the Collective Unconscious*. Princeton: Princeton University Press.

Keefer, B. and Schooler, J.E. (2000) *Telling the Truth to Your Adopted or Foster Child*. Westport: Greenwood Publishing Group.

Kelly, R.J.A. (2005) *Motherhood Silenced: The Experience of Natural Mothers on Adoption Reunion*. Dublin: Liffey Press.

Kirk, H.D. (1984) *Shared Fate: A Theory and Method of Adoptive Relationships*. British Columbia: Ben Simon Publications.

Larkin, P. (2003) *Collected Poems*. London: Faber and Faber.

Lawless, S. (2016) *Adoption Stories*. Dublin: Carnegie Hill Publishing.

Lifton, B.J. (2010) 'Ghosts in the Adopted Family' in *Psychoanalytic Inquiry*, (30): 71–79.

Lifton, B.J. 1988). *Lost and Found: The Adoption Experience*. New York: Harper and Row Publishers.

Macavie, G.A. (2014) 'Simply an American Now' in Myung-Ja, et al. (eds.) *Adoptionland: From Orphans to Activists*. US: Against Child Trafficking Publishers.

Martin, E. A. (ed.) (2007) *Oxford Concise Medical Dictionary*. Oxford: Oxford University Press.

Megan, K. (2013). 'Yale Expert Says Teaching About Emotions Reduces Bullying' in *The Hartford Courant*. Available from: http://articles.courant.com/2013-11- 22/news/hc-emotional-intelligence-1123-20131122_1_emotional- intelligence-school-climate-marc-brackett

Melosh, B. (2002) *Strangers and Kin: The American Way of Adoption*. Massachusetts: Harvard University Press.

Miller, A. (2008) *The Drama of Being a Child*. London: Virago Press.

Moran, R.A. (1994) 'Stages of Emotion: An Adult Adoptee's Post Reunion Perspective' in *Child Welfare League of America*, 73(3): 249–260.

Neil, E. (2009) 'The Corresponding Experiences of Adoptive Parents and Birth Relatives in Open Adoptions' in Wrobel, G.M. & Neil, E. (eds.) *International Advances in Adoption Research for Practice*. Chichester: Wiley-Blackwell.

References

Oakwater, H. (2012) *Bubble Wrapped Children: How Social Networking is Transforming the Face of 21ˢᵗ Century Adoption.* London: MX Publishing.

O'Connor. G. (2012) 'Breaking the Code of Silence: The Irish and Drink' in *Irish America.* Available from: http://irishamerica.com/2012/01/breaking-the-code-of-silence-the-irish-and-drink/

O'Donnell, M. (1998) *Unlegendary Heroes.* Ireland: Salmon Poetry.

O'Shea, M. T., Collins, C. and Bourke, J. (2017) 'Post-placement intercountry adoption: GP's raise concerns' in *Forum,* 34 (6): 14–16.

Oxford Concise Medical Dictionary (2007) Martin, E. A. (ed.) Oxford: Oxford University Press.

Register, C. (1991) *Are Those Kids Yours? American Families with Children Adopted from Other Countries.* New York: The Free Press.

Register, C. (2005) *Beyond Good Intentions – A Mother Reflects on Raising Internationally Adopted Children.* St Paul: Yeong & Yeong Book Company.

Riley, D. and Meeks, J. (2006) *Beneath the Mask: Understanding Adopted Teens.* Burtonsville: CASE Publications.

Robinson, Burns E. (2003) *Adoption and Loss: The Hidden Grief.* Christies Beach: Clova Publications.

Rogers, C. (1961) *On Becoming a Person.* New York: Mariner Books.

Rothman, B.K. (1989) *Recreating Motherhood.* New York: W.W. Norton & Co.

Ruiz, D.M. (1997) *The Four Agreements.* California: Amber-Allen Publishing.

Rutter, M. et al. (2009) 'Effects of Profound Early Institutional Deprivation: An Overview of Findings from a UK Longitudinal Study of Romanian Adoptees' in Wrobel, G.N. & Neil, E. (eds.) *International Advances in Adoption Research for Practice.* Chichester: Wiley-Blackwell.

Ryan, D. (2012) *The Spinning Heart.* Dublin: Doubleday Ireland.

Silverstein, D. N., and Kaplan, S. (1982) *Lifelong Issues in Adoption,* American Adoption Congress 2018. Available from: https://www.americanadoptioncongress.org/grief_silverstein_article.php

Soll, J. 'Terror Is Non-Negotiable' in Adoption Healing (website). Available from: www.adoptionhealing.com /terror is non-negotiable.

Sugarman, L. (2001) *Life-Span Development: Frameworks, Accounts and Strategies.* Hove: Psychology Press.

Szalavitz, M. and Perry, B. (2010) *Born For Love: Why Empathy is Essential – and Endangered.* New York: Harper Collins.

Trollope, J. (2004). *Brother and Sister.* London: Transworld Publishers.

Verrier, N. (1993) *The Primal Wound: Understanding the Adopted Child.* Baltimore: Gateway Press.

References

Watt, A. (2011) 'Building Attachment is the First Step to Becoming a "Forever Daddy"', *The Guardian* (London), 6 January 2011.

Winterson, J. (2011) *Why Be Happy When You Could Be Normal?* London: Vintage Books.

Wolff, J. (2010) *Secret Thoughts of an Adoptive Mother.* Honolulu: Vista Communications.

Woititz, J. G. (1983) *Adult Children of Alcoholics.* Florida: Health Communications Inc.

Zayd, D. I. (2012) 'The New Abolition: Ending Adoption in Our Time' in Myung J., Potter, M.A. and Allen, L.V. (eds.) *Adoptionland: From Orphans to Activists.* US: Against Child Trafficking Publishers.

USEFUL SERVICES

Barnardos Post Adoption Service:
www.barnardos.ie

The Adoption Authority of Ireland:
www.aai.gov.ie

International Adoption Search Birth Families:
www.internationaladoptionsearch.com

C.A.S.E. Adoption Support:
http://adoptionsupport.org/store/w-i-s-e-up/